LIVING TO 99

YAFFA

MERAJ PUBLISHING

All words copyright © 2025
All rights reserved.
Published in 2025 by Meraj Publishing
1st Edition

Illustrations copyright © 2025
This is a work of creative nonfiction and memoir. It reflects the author's present recollections of experiences over time. Some parts or names have been fictionalized in varying degrees, for various purposes.

No part of this book may be reproduced or used in any manner without written permission of the copyright owner except for the use of quotations in a book review. For more information, address:
info@merajpublishing.com

ISBN: 979-8-9925727-0-4 (Paperback)
ISBN: 979-8-9925727-1-1 (Ebook)

Cover, Illustrations, and Calligraphy by Yaffa AS
Editing by Khaled A.
Layout by Andrea Ramos Campos
merajpublishing.com

Previous publications by Yaffa:

Blood Orange
Inara: Light to Utopia
Desecrated Poppies
Whispers Beneath the Orange Grove

For the souls whose hearts open in awe of divine spirit and who dream of liberation in defiance of oppression.

Introduction	15

Chapter 1: Big Picture 33

    1 Allah: The God... 35
    69 Al-Qaader: The Most Able..................................37
    74 Al-Aakher: The Last &.. 39
    73 Al-Awwal: The First.. 39
    62 Al-Mumeet: The Giver of Death........................ 42
    61 Al-Muhyi: The Giver of Life................................ 44
    55 Al-Mateen: The Firm &....................................... 47
    54 Al-Qawi: The Strong One.................................. 47
    63 Al-Hayy: The Everlasting/The Living................49
    4 Al-Malik: The Ruler... 52
    6 As-Salam: The Giver of Peace...........................54
    51 Ash-Shaheed: The Witness.............................. 58
    101 Al-Mubeen: The Manifest............................... 61
    13 Al-Baari: The Maker.. 63
    32 Al-Khabeer: The All Knowing............................ 65
    29 Al-Hakam: The Judge &.................................... 67
    30 Al-Adl: The Just... 67

Chapter 2: Community Care..69

    100 Al-Qayoom: The Self-Sustaining..................... 70
    81 Al-Muntaqim: The Avenger............................... 76
    102 Al-Musta'an: The One Who Is Called Upon For Help.. 79
    91 Ad-darr: The One Who Harms........................... 81
    57 Al-Hameed: The All Praiseworthy......................85

    41 Al-Haseeb: The Reckoner or Bringer of Judgement. 87
    27 As-Samee': The All Hearing.. 89
    28 Al-Baseer: The All Seeing...92
    33 Al-Haleem The Forbearing One................................... 95
    35 Al-Ghafoor: The All-Forgiving..97
    82 Al-Afu: The Forgiver... 100
    36 Ash-Shakoor: The Most Grateful................................. 103
    18 Ar-Razaqq: The All Provider.. 107

Chapter 3: Divine Values.. 109
    85 Dhul-Jallal Wal-Ikram: The Lord of Majesty and
    Generosity... 110
    95 Al-Badee': The Initiator, The Originator, or The
    Incomparable.. 114
    75 Ath-Thaher: The Visible/The Manifest........................117
    39 Al-Hafeez: The Preserver.. 119
    11 Al-Mutakabir:
    The Majestic..122
    105 Aalam Alghayb Wal-Shahada: The Knower of The
    Unseen and The Witnessed.. 124
    13 Al-Baari: The Maker..128
    15 Al-Ghaffar: The Ever Forgiving..................................... 130
    19 Al-Fattah: The Opener..131

Chapter 4: Who is Allah?.. 135
    67 Al-Ahad: The One and Only One &............................. 136
    66 Al-Wahed: The One.. 136
    92 An-Nafi: The Benefactor.. 139
    48 Al-Wadood: The Loving/Kind One............................142

100 Al-Maajid: The Glorious, The Illustrious................... 144

49 Al-Majeed: The All Glorious..146

68 As-Samad:
The Everlasting/
The Eternal.. 147

96 Al-Baqi: The One Who Remains............................... 149

12 Al-Khaliq: The Creator.. 151

37 Al-Aliyy: The High..153

38 Al-Kabeer: The Most Great....................................... 155

65 Al-Waajid: The Finder..156

Chapter 5: Collectivism.. 159

52 Al-Haqq: The Truth... 160

83 Ar-Rauf: The Ever Compassionate......................... 162

40 Al-Muqeet: The All Nourisher/The All Sustainer........ 166

44 Ar-Raqeeb: The Watchful One................................ 168

7 Al-Mu'min: The Grantor of Faith/The Grantor of
Security..172

8 Al-Muhaymin: The Protector...................................... 175

22 Al-Baasit The Expander/The Reliever &................... 177

21 Al-Qaabid The Restrainer...177

31 Al-Lateef: The Gentle One.......................................182

88 Al-Ghanii: The self-sufficient................................... 185

Chapter 6: Purpose...189

87 Al-Jamii: The Gatherer...190

86 Al-Muqsit : The One Who Is Just, The Equitable....... 192

17 Al-Wahabb: The Giver of All.................................... 194

25 Al-Muiz: The Giver of Honour... 196

97 Al-Warith: The Heir/The Successor............................. 199

24 Ar-Raafi: The Exalter &... 202

23 Al-Khafid: The One Who Humbles........................... 202

45 Al-Mujeeb: The One Who Answers........................ 204

47 Al-Hakeem: The All Wise.. 206

20 Al-Aleem: The All Knowing..................................... 208

103 Badi'us- Samaawaati wal-Ard: The Originator of the Heavens and the Earth.. 210

104 Fatir Alsamawat Wal'ard: Creator of the heavens and the earth... 210

43 Al-Kareem: The Most Generous.............................. 213

84 Malik Al-Mulk: The Ruler of All Creation................. 216

Chapter 7: Non-Attachment.. 219

56 Al-Waliyy: The Guardian, The Caretaker................. 220

76 Al-Baten: The Hidden... 223

90 Al-Maani: The One Who Prevents......................... 225

77 Al-Waali: The Guardian (Mother)............................ 229

89 Al-Mughni: The Enricher.. 231

9 Al-Azeez: The Almighty.. 234

16 Al-Qahhar: The One That Has Control of All........... 236

58 Al-Muhsee: The Assessor... 242

14 Al-Musawer: The Fashioner of Forms..................... 244

72 Al-Muakher: The Delayer &.................................... 247

71 Al-Muqadem: The Advancer................................... 247

99 As-Sabur: The Patient One..................................... 249

Chapter 8: Power - Claiming Humanity 253
    70 Al-Muqtader: The All Powerful..254
    78 Al-Muta'ali: The Most Exalted...................................... 257
    60 Al-Mueed: The Restorer...260
    59 Al-Mubdi': The Originator.. 263
    10 Al-Jabbar: The Compeller/The Restorer.................264
    26 Al-Mudhil: The Giver of Disgrace................................268
    50 Al-Baa'ith: The Restorer of Life...................................270
    5 Al-Qudoos: The Most Holy...272
    42 Al-Jaleel: The Most High/Honourable......................275
    53 Al-Wakeel: The One in Charge (Caretaker)............279
    46 Al-Waasi: The All Encompassing................................283

Chapter 9: Right Path.. 287
    98 Ar-Rashid: The Right Path..288
    34 Al-Atheem: The Great...294
    94 Al-Hadi: The One Who Guides................................... 296
    93 An-Noor: The Light.. 298
    3 Ar-Raheem: The Most Compassionate/The All Merciful &... 301
    2 Ar-Rahman: The Most Merciful/The Almighty............301
    80 At-Tawab: The Ever Accepting of Repentance..... 305
    79 Al-Barr: The Source of All Goodness and Kindness. 307

Afterword...309
About the Author...316
About Meraj Publishing...319

Throughout the book, you'll find QR codes for art that accompanies each chapter. You can the art here:

https://www.merajpublishing.com/living-to-99

Introduction

Art by Yaffa AS

1. At a future event, a participant will raise their hand and say, "I don't agree with every definition in this book."

I ask, "what were you looking for when you picked up *Living to 99?*"

"I wanted a guide to the definitions of the 99 Names of Allah to help me become a better Muslim," they say.

"I honor that you were searching for definitions, and this book is not about that. This book is a compilation of reflections about the 99 Names of Allah, not a dictionary or scholarly manual about the 99 names. These are my personal reflections, layered between my positionality of lived and professional experiences. This book is not a religious text by any means. Some of these reflections go into definitions and etymology. However, I do not claim to be an expert on the nuance and the layers of complexity that exist in the Arabic language. I wrote and now share this book because..."

Once upon a time, on Valentine's Day in 2016, I wrote an introduction to my 99 names of Allah countdown to spring that I had done earlier that year. It was written and saved on a drive, but I did not return to it until after writing a new introduction. I wrote the new introduction the week of Oct 7th, 2024, the one year anniversary.

The years 2015 and 2016 were what I refer to as the grappling years. 2017 was the year of fully falling back into the abyss, while 2018 was climbing out. 2019 and 2020 were all about rebuilding, whereas 2021 was my year of rest. 2022 was the year for family caretaking. This was all leading up to the fall 2023, when all my training kicked in to respond to the genocide in Palestine post Oct 7th, 2023.

Every year served a purpose, and before the fall of 2017, I was truly trying in 2015 and 2016. I almost cry writing this reflection thinking of the countless people — young, queer, trans, disabled, Muslim — who are also truly trying, not realizing that no matter what they do, oppressive systems will still create barriers on their journeys.

At the time, I was grappling with what life is meant to look like for someone like me, especially since no one around me looked or felt like me. I tried to make some semblance of a life where the people I knew interpersonally and professionally were not capable of holding, not just me, but anyone at the margins of marginalization. To be clear, these were not white-cis-straight people, and I was not attempting to assimilate into whiteness, cis-ness, straightness, or any of the other systems.

As I slipped farther into the abyss, I became resentful, but since I was in an abusive community at the time, where it was not safe to present that resentment direction, I turned the resentment towards the past.

In a lot of ways, those years outline my journey. I was born a light in an abyss; I scrambled out; I tried grappling with what I thought was the world I wanted, then I crashed back. I haven't left the abyss in the last few years. I am one with the abyss. I am also of the light. I hover within and above the light and the abyss. And both the abyss and light serve me. When I look back at this journey of reclamation, I think about the 99 names of Allah. In late 2015, I was feeling spiritually disconnected, not from The Divine, but from The Divine's creation. To support myself on this journey, I did a daily reflection, counting down to spring. I attempted to connect with The Divine's creation, but I connected with who I am instead. And through that connection, I reconnected with the creation. The 99 names reminded me of who I am, who I can be, who I will be, who I am meant to be, especially beyond the privileged gaze (the way the most privileged want us to be).

As I write this and read other things I've written (sometimes things that contradict one another), I also recognize that spirit is not a doorway. Spirit surrounds us at all times. If we're only looking at what's in front of us, we only see a small part of it and miss everything else. In one moment, I could question spirit. In another, I could genuinely believe I have never questioned spirit. Sometimes, I am part of spirit. And other times, spirit is so much more than anything that can ever be within me. The list goes on and on. To me, the 99 names are different layers to spirit, allowing me to see and feel spirit. Spirit to me is everything that exists beyond a single individual or presence.

Living to 99 is a project I have yearned to return to the entire time, but it never quite worked out. I always wanted it released around Ramadan, and I always wanted it to be a love letter to the queer and trans Muslim community. I returned to it immediately after one year had passed since Oct 7th, 2023. It is not lost on me that I returned to this project at a time when I have felt incredibly disconnected from queer and trans Muslims, as well as other communities I was part of in general. Revisiting this project and reflecting on the 99 names has allowed me to reconnect spiritually with others in a multitude of ways. It also reminded me of the numerous ways and names our people have used to pray and remember The Divine, which is evident in the inclusion of more than 99 names of The Divine in this collection — besides the names highlighted in the Quran, many names were passed on to us, some being contested and negated, while others agreed upon. I am reminded again and again that the names, known and unknown, will find us when we need them most. This collection has 105 names in total.

> **2.** I am tired
> of violence
> from States
> built to be violent
> and from communities
> who want to be
> States themselves
>
> - Mx. Yaffa from *Sage (2025)*

I understand religious trauma. I still feel the way teachers and baba twisted my ear whenever I was not the "best" Muslim. If I focus enough, I can still hear their words, telling me I am a sinner, hooker, hoe, disgusting, and ugly. If I lay in the sun long enough, I remember that I have been told countless times that someone like me is meant to go to Hell. I got these messages from other Muslims, as well as people following different faiths: Christians, Jews, Hindus, even Buddhists. I have even received them from atheists who don't believe in hell to begin with, yet somehow, they thought I was meant to be there. Perhaps I'm lucky that I was born equally hated by all, not from one religion, sect, or practice.

I was enamored by Allah. At four years old, visiting Seedo's land in Jordan for the first time, an acre of a wheatfield surrounded by mountains and stretching as far as the eye can see, felt like I was in Janna. I understood Allah most in that moment. I experienced an extent of joy my body could not contain. I ended up peeing myself while running through the field.

This memory is on my mind often because it encompasses all the complex emotions of my life: joy after running in nature for the very first time, shame and fear after peeing myself, loneliness after no one noticed, and maturity after feeling my actions were silly (unbecoming). I was a four-year-old internally shamed away from ever being a child — there were obviously external factors at play here, but they were not as powerful as what I could bring into my own bodymind. If I weren't an adult prior to this moment, running through the field then was the moment I became an adult. And if I weren't a child before that moment, then that was when I became a child. My entire childhood filled the space, a mere acre of land. On that acre, my childhood remained. Perhaps it still remains.

Ten years after running through it home is that field to me, both in my mind and later in my body, especially the few weeks after we moved to Jordan.. Some days, I yearn to purchase that house — stolen by my uncle — and make it home again. But the field is gone. All that's left is one acre, split between a house and trees that have reclaimed themselves since Seedo's passing.

I walked away an adult, truly knowing Allah for the first time in this life. Praying, reading the Quran, fasting, and other religious practices have never been difficult for me. I understood prayer. I loved rolling the words of the Quran on my tongue. I savored the dryness of a compassionate tongue while fasting. And I knew how to reach out to Allah, knowing that Allah was closer to me than the vein I could not remember on the side of my neck. I asked for a brother. I asked for food. I asked for someone to play with. I asked to stop crying. I asked for no one to notice when I peed myself (FYI, it only happened twice when I was 4 and 7). I asked for everything.

The Islam I was taught stated that our connection with Allah is strengthened when we move past our egos. Perhaps it was through the Islam of poverty I also learned Allah is The Only One you can count on. Perhaps it's because no human ever came when I called that I developed this strong bond with The Divine. Perhaps it was because when humans came, I was beat, yelled at, or raped as a child. Either way, my body was all I had, all there was to this adult living in a child's body.

Here is where I feel different from others who have experienced religious trauma. Where others would blame Allah or other higher entities, I blamed humans, and over time, I learned to specifically blame systems of oppression. I have never blamed Allah. I do not feel entitled to Allah recreating the world for me, dismissing other people's realities. I have always known that I own my life, in beautiful non-attached ways. If those around me and I have not done the work to build a better world, are we ready for Allah to grant it? The answer is no.

I often ask the audience during my book talks and panels if they feel ready for a world without systemic oppression. Would they know what to do? Out of tens of thousands of people I have asked this question, no one said they were ready. If I asked Allah for a world free of systemic oppression, what good will that do, especially if all humans know is to replicate the systems of oppression we are currently living in?

I do not wish oppression on anyone. I do not wish on anyone to endure what I have endured in my life, let alone a child. And I am grateful for the life I have been gifted, a life that from the youngest of ages broke me down into nothing. My mind moved into adulthood through joy, followed by shame and fear. My body moved into adulthood starving, grieving countless lives, and lacking a home on the borders of the Syrian Revolution — psychosis and shame filled every part of my soul.

I find that I understand Allah when I understand Allah as the unknown, more so than the known. I feel Allah in nature, in stars, in my heartbeat, in everything known to me, but I understand Allah more in what is unknown to me. This understanding is the building block for non-attachment. I am currently writing this on a plane, flying from Ohlone land to Tungva land. I had planned to be early to the airport, but I arrived late. I refused to be stressed as I raced to check in my bags, knowing that what was destined to happen would happen. My bags could not be checked in, and the lovely attendant asked if I wanted to be moved to the non-stop flight instead of my current one with a layover. This delay allowed me to check in with a few individuals. These check-ins could not have waited. This is where I understand Allah. I can say that life is unfair, that Allah must be a horrible being because of my pain and all the pain out there, but the truth is that I am not that significant. I am not more important than eight billion humans and countless other beings.

In summer 2023, on my very first trip to Falasteen, a queer poet said she finally believed in Allah. She said there must be a sadistic creator to have envisioned this reality. I laughed — it's so easy to blame Allah instead of giving up a 401(k).

For me, I suppose, I really don't care whether or not someone believes in a higher power at all. I don't even care if you can feel any level of spirituality. What matters is how you move towards liberation. Organized religions and non-believers claim they are the only power in charge of moving towards liberation. Yet, they are often the ones resisting liberation by constricting entry points into connection.

There are countless entry points and pathways to move us towards liberation, all leading to the same endpoint. Believing only one pathway can exist creates barriers from reaching liberation, which ultimately means you are not committed to liberation.

If you aim to create barriers to liberation, then you are supporting fascism. It's that simple.

I was recently asked what role religion played in collective liberation. I asked whether they meant spirituality or religion because I view them as separate entities. Religion can be a part of spirituality, but spirituality extends far beyond any dogma. Spirituality is connection, the connection with humans you will never meet and will never share a timeline. It is the connection with land, even if you have no "claim" to said land. It is the connection to stars and wisdom that exists in forests that we can't comprehend. I said that there may be other ways that don't include any spirituality, but I find it very difficult to imagine collective liberation without spirituality. To me, spirituality is the building block of collectivism, and there is no collective liberation without collectivism.

There is a lot that can be said about how The Divine has been weaponized to move us away from The Divine for the short term benefit for a few, but that can only occur when we do not have access to ways of knowledge that affirm our connection with The Divine. There is a reason that at every stage of religious corruption, those in power will punish education, community conversations, questions that ask beyond what they themselves have determined as right or wrong. The Divine asks us, as individuals and communities, to interrogate this compass of morality through these names again and again as we live our lives. The Divine has given us a blueprint and free will to determine how we move through our lives. Free will does not imply being absolved of consequence, for our actions have consequences in this life and in what comes next. The Divine, through these names, made our purpose (steward the land and care for one another) and the paths to achieve this purpose (community care, love, compassion, non-attachment, understanding humanity and divinity (power)) clear. The Divine also made it abundantly clear that we are all connected (every living being, not just humans), and that every step we take on any path impacts everyone and everything. Our purpose is not an individual one — it can only be completed collectively.

Everything comes from The Divine (Al-Ahad and Al-Samad).

Only Allah creates and is Original (Al-Badi and Al-Musawer).

If Allah wills it it shall be — no one supersedes The Divine (Power)(Al-Qahhar).

Allah has embedded all creation with the essence of The Divine (love, patience, forgiveness, grace, majesty).

Allah has tasked us with roles and responsibilities (stewarding the land and caring for one another)(collectivism)(Al-Jami).

Allah has given us glimpses into things that are beyond us — Only Allah Knows All (non-attachment)(Al-Aleem).

I wrote this book as a love letter to queer and trans people looking to ground in spirituality in a world where unfortunately many spiritual places tell us that we are not compatible with divinity. But we are divine.

I wrote the following poem for *desecrated poppies* and I can't think of a better way to start this collection.

        they hate us
    because we remind
   them of the divine and
  they realize they're nothing
        like Them

        they envy us
   because we're the
 essence of the divine and
they feel helpless in their
         void

        they kill us
   because it's the
  closest to the divine
   they could ever

get

they hate us
they envy us
they kill us

the result is
the same

we are hated
we are envied
we are murdered
we are divine

Chapter 1: Big Picture

Art by Yaffa AS

1 Allah: The God

We are asked to refer to Allah through the names gifted to us.
We are also warned about abusing the names.

وَلِلَّهِ ٱلْأَسْمَآءُ ٱلْحُسْنَىٰ فَٱدْعُوهُ بِهَا ۖ وَذَرُواْ ٱلَّذِينَ يُلْحِدُونَ فِىٓ أَسْمَـٰٓئِهِۦ ۚ سَيُجْزَوْنَ مَا كَانُواْ يَعْمَلُونَ [1]

Allah has the Most Beautiful Names. So call upon Him by them, and keep away from those who abuse His Names. They will be punished for what they do.

The names of Allah illustrate different pathways to The Right Path, every step along the way. To abuse any of the steps is to abuse them all. To weaponize the names, their meanings, the stories behind them, or anything they might imply is absolutely prohibited. Many are taught that Allah is constantly looking to punish us by only sharing a very limited interpretation of a few names of Allah. To me, this includes individuals who weaponize the gifts gifted to us. To

---

[1] https://quran.com/en/al-araf/180

weaponize mercy, love, compassion, faith, safety, or any of the other attributes across any spiritual faith or any aspect of life, is an abuse of the 99 names.

I share these reflections recognizing the weight of misrepresenting The Divine. I share them anyway. I pray for growth, accountability, and to never assume that I am any more or less than I am.

69 Al-Qaader: The Most Able

I feel a sense of warmth when I think of Allah. Not because of what Allah can grant me, but because I feel a sense of warmth every time I connect with anything beyond my ego. I do not believe that Allah is The Most Able because I or anything else was created. I believe that Allah is The Most Able, regardless of any expectation and desire.

Palestinians (and potentially other Arabs) have a saying, "Maktoob," which means it is written — it is destiny. Destiny is not this distanced concept; destiny is every breath lived and unlived. The root of the word Qaader — Qadar (قدر) — is the same word we use for destiny. The Most Able is The One who defines our destiny. The word Qaader has movement within it. It's not that Allah is The Most Able, it's that Allah utilizes that ability in ways we can't even begin to imagine —

and I don't yearn to. I savor knowing that Al-Qaader takes care of us, and that's enough for me.

We — humans — are destiny in the making; we are Allah's creation. We are defined, honored, and elevated through The Most Able. That knowledge always makes me feel a sense of warmth.

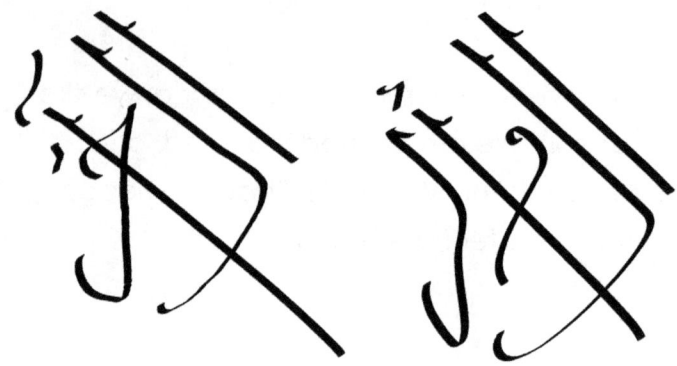

74 Al-Aakher: The Last &
73 Al-Awwal: The First

Allah carries opposing names, names on both ends of a binary, such as The First and The Last. As I write this, I reflect on what the purpose of us knowing this is. We know Allah is Al-Baqqi, The One Who Remains, but it is not enough to remain. The First and The Last are a promise — there is nothing before and nothing after Al-Aakher. Al-Awwal is the entire circle of being. There is nothing outside of Al-Awwal, there is only Al-Aakher. Nothing will exist after, and nothing has ever existed before. Everything within the circle that we call life is entirely Allah's. There is no shared creation. There is no shared ownership. There is nothing on the same level.

I remember the ridiculousness of shows like Supernatural (loved the show until this plot point), where the idea of Satan is equivalent to Allah, and in season 4 (I think) God disappears, just leaves it all behind as if any of it exists without Allah.

In Islam, when Iblis — the Islamic name for Satan (Shaitan) — decided not to bow to Adam, he asked Allah to allow him to lead humans astray. Iblis does not consider himself equal with Al-Awwal; Iblis knows that it is Al-Aakher's will that defines everything. Iblis is a creation of Al-Awwal and recognizes that he (Iblis) only exists within Allah's domain through Al-Aakher's grace. In Islam, Iblis is not a counterpart to Allah or even to Angels; Iblis is a creation like any other, no more and no less.

Everything starts and ends with Allah's will. We are gifted a small slice of time to make decisions and choose whether we move towards liberation or towards injustice. But that decision is irrelevant in the scope of Allah's will. Our decisions do not and cannot harm Allah. We can destroy this planet, fail in our purpose to steward land, care for one another, and Allah will still be The First and The Last. We are specs, barely particles in the scheme of an entire universe that we do not own.

62 Al-Mumeet: The Giver of Death

Death is not the opposite of life. Death is not even the absence of life. They are not two ends of an extreme. Death is very much a part of life because death comes from Al-Mumeet. Death is a release — it is the opening to a next chapter or a sequel of sorts instead of the end of a book. Our lives are filled with shocks to our systems and pathways in life. We may feel we are moving in a certain direction and then find ourselves shocked into another. Death is the ultimate shock to our lives. This shock is necessary for our growth and movement towards self-actualization.

Within my practice of Islam, I believe that the descriptors of Heaven and Hell are just of what it feels like to be closer to or farther from Al-Mumeet. I believe this shock is still about our growth, attempting to always move us closer to Al-Mumeet. Not everyone takes the invitation of the shocks in our lives to move closer to Al-Mumeet — many will move away. But there is always another shock. On and on they go, until we finally reach self-actualization.

61 Al-Muhyi: The Giver of Life

Al-Muhyi is the only one who can truly give us life, on a physical level (heart beating), spiritual level (connection to other beings), and emotional level (feeling life). Sometimes, it feels as if other living beings are able to give us life. It could be a loved one, land, ancestors, stars It could be anything. I could feel inspired, joyful, angry, sad, and so many other things around others.

But only Al-Muhyi can give us life — everything else is just a feeling, and feelings are temporary. Feeling alive is not the same as being given life. How many of us have fallen in love with the wrong people? (no judgements — I've been there (am I still here?))

The life Al-Muhyi gives us is incomparable to anything else — it is perfect!

What is life? What does it mean to be given life?

I think about how every doctor who has "saved" my life was only undoing harm done by another doctor. I think about all the mental health billboards and fundraising campaigns that ask you to "save" lives. I think about evacuations from genocide zone and campaigns to end genocide that often claim to "save" lives.

As a peer support specialist and death worker, I know that my role is not to "save" anyone, and I know within my body and soul that that's not something I can ever be capable of. Some people I support might place that on me and say I "saved" them, but I know the truth. I cannot gift life, nor can I take it unless it is willed.

Al-Muhyi grants us life in all the dimensions of life. To me, that includes physical life, emotional life, spiritual life, and dimensions beyond what I am able to understand but know exist.

I think of everything given to us by Al-Muhyi as a gift. Life is a gift — not in a anti-suicide kind of way; rather, life is purposeful. Purpose exists in everything, including death. Life is a gift from beyond us, and like any gift, sometimes we don't want it or would rather something different. I think that's okay. That's a part of it. Sometimes a gift needs to sit with us for years before we're ready to claim it. Life is a responsibility. To be alive is to claim purpose: to steward the land and care for one another. To live is to claim so much, and sometimes we're not ready, and that's okay. The gift does not change because we haven't claimed it — what changes is our relationship with it.

I choose everyday to have a purposeful relationship with this gift. I choose to live with purpose and to die with purpose, and I know that I control nothing beyond my immediate choices.

55 Al-Mateen: The Firm & 54 Al-Qawi: The Strong One

The word strength comes from "to fort," which means to be firm and not malleable. To be weak is to be malleable.

Humans love emulating strength, assuming that power comes from being firm, when in fact true power comes from weakness. When we are malleable, we are able to expand our power — we are able to grow and move towards self-actualization. Allah is The Only One who is Al-Qawi, who operates from that space of strength because Allah does not need to grow. Al-Qawi does not need to be flexible or malleable. But we do. Al-Qawi is perfection at a level that we can't even comprehend because it is not a level that we can ever achieve. The weaker, more vulnerable we are, the more we are able to truly expand to witness Al-Mateen/Al-Qawi more and more.

Al-Mateen and Al-Qawi both refer to Allah's strength. However, Al-Mateen is about how unwavering that strength is. Allah's strength is not negotiable. Al-Qawi alone implies that Allah is The Strong One, while Al-Mateend expands the definition to infinitely and everlastingly strong. Al-Mateen's strength knows no bounds; it is simply unwavering.

63 Al-Hayy: The Everlasting/The Living

Are we alive? What does it mean to be alive? There are plenty of people who believe we are not, a Matrix style existence of sorts — we are of oblivion, are oblivion, and return to oblivion. There are others who believe our existence is accidental and carries no weight beyond a temporary moment of being. People have debated the existence of souls and life forces for thousands of years. Without a soul, a source of life, are we alive? What does it mean to be alive?

To me, I believe in a singular life force, Allah, Al-Hayy. It is our connection with Al-Hayy that makes us alive. We are alive because we are an extension of Al-Hayy, and without that connection, we are no longer alive. In some cultures, there's a concept of being without a soul —or soulloss— that in many ways represents being so far away from Al-Hayy, that you are no longer operating from a place of living. In

Arabic, we say Daya'a Roho — They lost their soul. More recently, these terms are used to describe pro-genocide individuals and those conducting genocide — they are soulless.

Life comes when we move towards Al-Hayy. It is not simply a feeling of being alive, it is a sensation that encompasses all sensations. When we connect fully, we reach enlightenment or self-actualization. People have gone to immense lengths to try to replicate this reality.

Everything connected to Al-Hayy is alive: the land, the sea, and every other form of creation we know of or will never cognize. When we connect with Al-Hayy's creation, we are able to connect deeper with Al-Hayy, for Al-Hayy is all around us.

As I write this, I am at the hot springs near Washoe Land. The sulfur-infused water is alive. The sky coated thickly with grey clouds is alive. The trees hovering above me are alive. The table I am writing on is made of wood that is alive in its own way. I am alive. The only thing not alive is the laptop on which I type. However, every hand – predominantly black and brown workers – who touched it during its manufacturing process **is** alive.

Even those committing genocide are alive — something so deep within them is still alive. When I interact with them, I feel a sense of sorrow for the part that is buried so far that it almost seems as if they are not alive at all, that they have never moved towards Al-Hayy.

4 Al-Malik: The Ruler

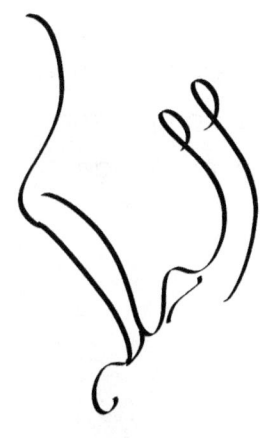

Al-Malik is a constant reminder of how petty and meaningless our human squabbles are. I am able to recognize the sadness in the billionaires, even as they attempt to kill us all. How sad must they be as merchants of pain and suffering.

One of my worst nightmares is giving someone a cold, the flu, COVID, or anything else that can be contagious. I don't care if someone in my life gives them to me, but not the other way around. I am not alone. I do everything I possibly can to protect others. I wonder what life would be like to know with certainty that millions died because of how you chose to live your life.

There can never be a ruler that compares to Al-Malik. Human rule, when built on supremacy, means you are a ruler through the suffering of others. Al-Malik is The Ruler who will always do right by us. Al-Malik is not The

Ruler *because* we suffer or have joy or anything else. Al-Malik is The Ruler. Period. There is no comparison, and there is no authority that can ever challenge Al-Malik.

6 As-Salam: The Giver of Peace

I studied conflict transformation and social justice for my Masters Degree. You probably don't hear me mentioning that very often. I did it to get a break, not because of any kind of career or learning aspirations. The program was filled with predominantly white women in their early 20's, who claimed they wanted to "infiltrate the FBI," and I would laugh at them and ask "you?" they agreed, but obviously I can't get to everyone.

Most of those kids ended up in state agencies, large NGOs, or other evil spaces. The program was run by one of the most fabulous individuals I know, but that didn't mean she could shield the group from other instructors who were very much only there for neo-liberal institutions paving the way for expanding and uplifting the white supremacist colonial project.

We talked about peace a lot. In particular, we talked about conflict and paving the road for peace. Although there was an acknowledgement that positive peace required dismantling the root causes, and at times there was a critique of the white supremacist colonial project and neo-liberal institutions, it offered zero possibilities into actually doing that work.

If we can agree that all conflict is stemming from systemic oppression, but we do not approach to dismantling systemic oppression, then what we're saying is there will never be peace because these systems will always be here, which is fundamentally false. No empire stands the test of time. No system of oppression is sustainable or sustained.

There is positive peace in the conflict sense, which happens after addressing the root causes of violence. Then there is the peace that exists through balance, and that would be referred to as inner peace in many spaces. To achieve societal positive peace, we must address the societal root cause of the challenges preventing positive peace. To achieve inner peace, we must address the root cause that exists within us as individuals — individual definition varies due to individualism, collectivism, or anywhere on the spectrum.

I was taught that Islam is a daily practice that promotes balance. In discussing As-Sabur, I mentioned the Sabr card in the Sufi Tarot. The Sabr card corresponded with the temperance card, which is the card for inner peace representing balance and harmony.

The Arabic word for peace, salam — our muslim greeting — is sin-lam-mim, which can translate to "whole" or "intact." When we say As-Salamu Alaikum, it is a promise that I mean you no harm and intent to leave you "whole". Peace is about being whole. Systemic oppression creates barriers to this peace but can not prevent it. Systemic oppression creates the circumstances to keep us away from ourselves and one another, yet systemic oppression fails.

We are whole because we were made whole. Being whole is beyond ableist understandings of functionality and body parts. You can rip me limb by limb, but I will remain whole. It has taken years to journey to the parts of myself that make me whole, and I have so much more travel to go through as I uncover more and more. Peace to me is learning that there is nothing I can ever find within me that is imperfect. It is perfect because it exists. Perfection is not a destination for me — perfection is a lifetime of growth and movement.

I am at peace at the beach, where I can connect with the four elements and spirit.

I am at peace writing these words.

I am working and growing to be at peace for as much of my day as I can, which doesn't mean avoiding my life, but it's rather about expanding peace to encompass more family and friends and movements.

51 Ash-Shaheed: The Witness

I have a complicated relationship with the word Al-Shaheed. We call our martyrs Shuhada (شهداء), the witnesses. Simultaneously, I have a beautiful relationship with it. It sounds beautiful and profound to honor people as witnesses when they are killed instead of just labeling them as victims. The complicated part comes from the fact that most communities do not know how to honor and hold death for what it is, and instead, focus on the injustice that leads to the death conflating the two. Death will always happen; there is no preventing it. Injustice is bad, and we work to eradicate it everywhere.

When one of my people is killed, they are witnessing injustice directly. In doing so, they ask us what we are doing to prevent this injustice in the future. They witness, so that we may act. They do not ask us to witness. They ask us to act, so that it never happens again. But we know that not everyone acts, regardless of how visible a genocide is. To be really honest, with the horrifying atrocities being committed, even I feel like I am not fully honoring my role. I am often asked at events about survivor's guilt, and my response usually is "who has time?" I, like many others, experience survivor's guilt. I honor it and move forward because I must — because the Shuhada demand actions, and not getting stuck in self-pity. I honor my humanity, that I will not act 100% of the time. I honor that I can refine my skills and work towards being more effective and strategic. At the end of the day, only Al-Shaheed perfectly witnesses all.

Al-Shaheed witnesses everything in existence and outside of it. There is nothing that is missed, all the moments we show up, and all the moments we do not act. The Shuhada of our world might not be able to see if we act or not, but Al-Shaheed witnesses all. Not only are we witnessed in our decisions, but in our entire decision-making process. There is no pretending like we did not know or did not know what to do. Al-Shaheed witnesses all.

I think about who I want to be witnessed as, knowing that there is no hiding, there is no denial. I aim to honor death and life, to witness and act, to grow and embody, and always move towards Al-Shaheed.

101 Al-Mubeen: The Manifest

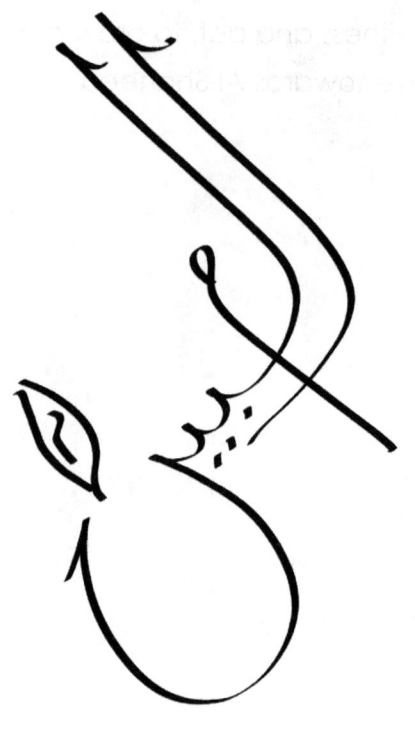

I have yet to meet someone who truly does not believe in any part of spirit. I have met many atheists, but they are people who talk about how the moon's cycles and their menstruation are connected; the ones who see their ancestors in the ocean and tears of loved ones; the ones who talk to trees on evening walks.

Al-Mubeen is all around us at all times. Al-Mubeen can be felt in looking up and noticing a parent and a child, both on their phone, and witnessing the loss of connection between them — yet they sit here, together, in silence. Al-Mubeen is in the two friends leaning on one another and clearly catching up for the first time in a while, joy heard in every word. Al-Mubeen is in the smiles, confused glances, and longing looks being exchanged between lovers and strangers.

Al-Mubeen is The Manifest and manifests in every interaction, whether we're paying attention or not. Before I knew Al-Mubeen in words and concepts, I knew Al-Mubeen in the smell of jasmine in the streets of Jordan, in wheatgrass fields, in smiles. Al-Mubeen is so close that, whether we open or close our eyes, we witness Al-Mubeen.

13 Al-Baari: The Maker

When I write a book, develop a curriculum, or create a piece of visual art, I am taking bits and pieces of things I have seen my entire life and things that may belong to ancestors, land, or a million other possible places. Nothing I "create" is unique or completely new — none of your favorite "creators" have created anything new. We all recycle different things, a reminder that "creation" in the human sense is always a collaborative process, even when working alone.

Al-Baari is The Only Original Maker, The Only Original Creator. Al-Baari creates from nothing — there is no influence, no recycling or upcycling, or anything else. Al-Baari creates uniquely in a way that we can never mimic, and in my opinion should never try.

I love that writing this book on my own in my apartment, or wherever I am, means that there are always countless others in these pages. Sometimes, that's actual collaboration, and mostly, it means that there are countless entities I do and don't know that are here writing this with me.

32 Al-Khabeer: The All Knowing

Khabeer comes from the word khabar, which can be translated to news or information. The word comes up most often in relation to news, or when asking someone to tell you things (asking for tea). Khabeer can be used for an expert in the field, someone who has a lot of information. I would be considered a Khabeer in many of the fields I am in: engineering, peer support, trauma healing, death work, birth work, management, non-profits, publishing, and organizing. As I picked up this project again, nine years after the original publication, I reread what I had written back then. Before a Trump presidency, COVID, OCt 7th, and although I was seen as an expert in many of the same areas above, the amount of growth I had to experience was immense, to the point that I would not share what I wrote back then unless to show how much I have grown. A Khabeer is not someone who knows everything. Rather, it is someone who has captured a certain amount of knowledge that is constantly continuing to develop and is positioned due to their own lived and professional experience (a lot of "experts" do not position themselves and view themselves as fully self-actualized beings but we can't all be perfect some people need to be problematic).

Al-Khabeer is The Only One who is in fact The All Knowing. The rest of us are in constant flux, growing as we experience the world, as others identify new knowledge areas and come to terms with what we know; what we thought we knew; and grow towards more refined knowledge. Al-Khabeer already knows everything. Al-Khabeer is The Only Expert in everything, no need for refinement or growth — something we will never be able to achieve. When we move towards knowledge, we move towards Al-Khabeer.

29 Al-Hakam: The Judge & 30 Al-Adl: The Just

I yearn for judgment. I yearn for an understanding of how my rough edges have interacted with others. I yearn for others to know how their rough edges have interacted with mine. I yearn for judgment from individuals I hope to never cross paths with but who have harmed everyone I know.

Only Al-Hakam knows all there is to know in creation to be able to stand between us all, in the complexity of harm that's possible. I'm talking about the smaller interpersonal harm and the larger harm where billions are harmed at the hands of one person. Al-Hakam is not corrupt within a system created by the individuals harming billions of us. Al-Hakam operates from a space beyond anything we can ever imagine, for Al-Hakam is Al-Adl, The Just.

Everything we can understand about justice is so limited in comparison. Often our visions of justice center the idea of pain, wanting others to experience the pain we're experiencing. Many versions of hell and heaven center this idea, but spreading pain is not justice and does not make us feel better. It can be cathartic, but its effects are short-lived. What would genuine justice look like for the people who started slavery? What would it look like for the individuals who started imperialism? What would it look like for the preacher who hijacked the words of Allah to abuse others?

There are countless forms of harm out there. Thinking of justice is a great practice, and I love that I don't actually know what justice looks like. I am limited in my being — what Al-Hakam is able to determine is beyond anything I could imagine and that brings immense warmth into my life. I can let go of the expectation that I need to know anything and instead know that genuine justice will happen.

Chapter 2: Community Care

Art by Yaffa AS

100 Al-Qayoom: The Self-Sustaining

I was 4 when I was abused by a neighbor.

I was 6 the first time a white woman called the cops on me.

I was 10 when I nearly cut off my finger and was told to never cry again — I didn't for over a decade.

I was 13 after one too many growth spurts and we couldn't afford clothes that fit me, so I convinced everyone that I was always warm and wore shorts and a t-shirt in the Canadian winter.

I was 14 when the frostbite nearly took my toes.

I was 16, nearly 17, when I left home and slept on park benches between two countries, avoiding as many people as I could.

I love my parents, and even they will acknowledge that they did not raise me, nor were they my caretakers. In exchange for food and housing, I was responsible for sisters I no longer talk to, grocery shopping for a family of 7-10 at different times, and raising three sisters I do talk to.

I have lived in three countries with my family and seven others alone.

I know abuse better than I know my body.

I don't know which hospital broke me. I don't know which time I should have gone to a hospital that didn't break my body.

I glued and taped the pieces of my body and mind together and filled it with spirit to be where I am today.

I am 32 when I feel fully supported for the first time. I am moving and friends tell me I'm not allowed to lift a single box, and that they hired trans people to pack and move my things while I go to acupuncture.

This is the first time I truly have a community I can rely on. For 32 years, I have been on my own — I have been proud of my ability to survive and even thrive. But I wasn't actually self-sustaining.

I was 2 when I disassociated and met Teta as she was dying on the ceiling of the grey living room.

I was 4 when the wheatgrass embraced me.

I was 6 when the sky and ocean carried me to safety.

I was 10 when I stopped fearing the dark and was called to pray 5 times a day.

I was 14 when I went North, the warmth healing my frostbite.

I was 17 when I grieved in graveyards in my mind.

I was at every age when spirit carried me.

I have never been alone.

I thought I could be self-sustaining like Allah as the flame on Mount Sinai speaking to Prophet Musa. The flame is independent of any external needs — it does not need wood or oil to burn or air to thrive. It exists outside of any factors that are necessary for fire to burn. Allah is Al-Qayyum The Self-Sufficient, there is nothing that Allah needs.

We, on the other hand, are not Self-Sustaining or Self-Sufficient, and we were never meant to be. If our role on this planet is to steward land, then even beyond our basic needs, we need one another to fulfill that purpose. I might be able to take care of a small plot of land, but land doesn't stop at an acre or a fence. Pretending as if our lives can exist within a border is individualistic. If where I am is not connected to where you are, then we will not steward this land.

I was talking to a dear friend recently, and I told him that I felt disconnected from nature, stars, spirits. I told him I used to hear and see them more. He said that maybe it's not that I'm disconnected from them; — rather, that they are carrying me and don't need to speak through me.

In the times when it feels like everything has fallen apart and everyone has abandoned us, Al-Qayoom still carries us. We can attempt to carry one another, but none of us are self-sustaining, and there will always be something missing. Al-Qayoom is The Self-Sustaining and carries us all, without a need for anything in return.

We are always carried, even when we deny that we are. We can move away from spirit; we can disbelieve that trees have feelings and wisdom that far surpass our own. Our denial does not define or affect Spirit. Al-Qayoom is Self-Sustaining regardless.

As I train communities on community support, we talk about times in our lives when others were supporting us, but that support was not felt and connected to. Our feelings of disconnection do not change that support was offered. Perhaps decades later we finally claim that support for what it is.

I hated my parents throughout high school. Now, I see everything they did with the little they had. They may not have been the ones to take me to hospitals when I needed it, held my hands, or hugged me. But they built a container for me to connect with Spirit everyday of my life.

I am forever grateful for their support.

We often look at sufficiency from a personal lens instead of a communal one. It is easier to recognize that we need one another for our survival — still does not happen enough, but to recognize that I need you because of something much greater than just me is spirituality. Collectivism is recognizing that we need one another for our survival — in one way or another. Spirituality is the connection to a purpose beyond any ego.

81 Al-Muntaqim: The Avenger

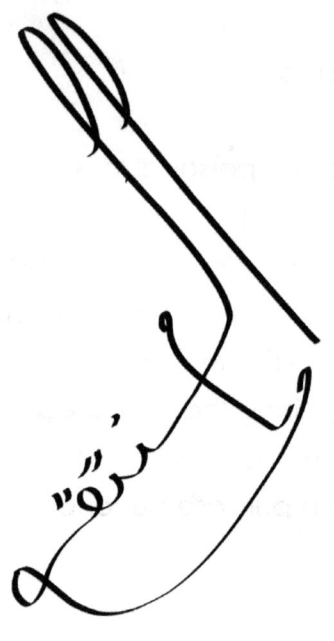

I have wanted to hurt people who have hurt me. I have wanted vengeance. I want it now, even after years of practicing transformative justice. 16 months into the most visible genocide we've ever had on this planet, nearly 2 years into the genocide in Sudan, 7 years into the genocide in Congo — I want vengeance. And I also know that I do not. Vengeance is a way of transferring pain and assuming we've resolved it. I want Justice. I want to build a world where genocide can never exist. But not everyone will see justice, not everyone will be avenged even if we wanted to avenge them.

In my organizing and philosophy in life, I believe nothing is wasted. It does not just disappear because someone has died without justice. Even when the worst things happen, I can still utilize them as a spring to move towards collective liberation. When a crisis occurs, we move towards collective liberation. When a conflict arises, we move towards collective liberation. When bad organizing happens, we move toward collective liberation. When the state tries to kill us, we move toward collective liberation.

I feel the same about the Divine, The Avenger will avenge us. Nothing is lost to The Avenger. It can be lifetimes later, but justice will be served — nothing is lost or wasted.

In my work, I see harmed individuals who are looking to spread that pain — in many instances, that pain is then spread to individuals and communities who have nothing to do with the original harm, and, in fact, are often trying to support the harmed. We see this everyday; community members direct violence towards their own communities because systems of oppression terrorize us. The truth is if we wanted to avenge and seek true justice, we would not know how. Even the transformative justice practice is not perfect. We do the best we can, but it's never 100%. I have worked with dozens of communities around accountability processes, and every single time, they look different, and there is no guaranteeing how the process will flow. Most times we enter a process with one harm in mind, but in reality, it's something completely different. Sometimes, the process doesn't end in a way that many would assume is closure. Sometimes, the community is not there by the end of it. And sometimes, the most magical things happen — communities are built; people who haven't spoken to each other in decades are reuniting for the first time; healing rules, and the things that come to life beyond it shake me to my core.

Like everything else, only Allah is perfect! We are human, and we are meant to be imperfect. This imperfection, this lack of knowing what is to come and submitting to it through non-attachment, is how we grow. As we move through imperfect ways of seeking justice, we learn to truly move towards justice. Nothing is wasted.

102 Al-Musta'an: The One Who Is Called Upon For Help

I know too many people who refuse to ask for help when they really need it. I used to think I could not ask for help. After further reflection, I realize that it is not that I do not ask for help — I ask for help, but help is rarely extended. I am not an easy person to support — my life being a brand of chaos that most people can not comprehend supporting me through.

Support is a language of its own. We all have our own ways of communicating the need for support and receiving it. Calling for help from other humans does not always mean we will receive support or feel supported. Support is a multi-step process, except when we turn to Al-Musta'an for support. Al-Musta'an supports us in ways that we don't even know we need, in ways that speak to parts of us that we may not be connected with.

The relationship with Al-Musta'an for me is a beautiful way of connecting support with other people and entities around me. If I can hold that, I am always receiving support from Al-Musta'an in ways that are moving me towards The Right Path, whether I know it or not. This enables me to! become more receptive to support from everyone and everything else.

When I am in nature, I am supported in ways I do not know yet. When friends support me in a way that doesn't align with what I initially needed, that does not mean I am not supported. It might be that they're supporting a part of me I have yet to be fully connected with. We are always supported.

91 Ad-darr: The One Who Harms

Who has the authority to harm you, or me? To harm anyone?

For many of us, harm is something we experience daily. Within my world of conflict transformation and transformative justice, the question of what constitutes harm is integral. Naming something as harm does not objectively make it harmful. A feeling of harmfulness is different from the reality of being harmed.

Every day we are gaslit by over a dozen systems of oppression creating every circumstance for us to disconnect from our body, mind, and spirit. Most of us can barely name our feelings during the best of times, let alone the worst. Yet, we pretend to know and understand harm within the plethora of other feelings that we have. Harm is real and exists along a spectrum of intensity, motivations, and results. It fascinates me that even etymologically the word harm — in various languages — is incredibly vague. The word "'harm'" tells us nothing except that harm was done or someone is harmful or harmless.

Within my organizing and community care work, individuals will view things like discomfort and accountability as harm. Does that mean when harm is felt, harm has occurred? What then is the difference between the feeling of harm and the realities of being harmed? Surely discomfort to healthy behavior is not the same as rape. However, language-wise, they are very much occupying the same category of harm. Since harm is vaguely defined, it allows the most privileged to claim that they are the ones being harmed, when, in reality, the most marginalized are harmed in every way. Often our existence is the catalyst for said harm — many of us need trigger warnings to share any part of our stories to the same people who benefit from the suffering we have endured.

Yet, I assert, again and again, that harm is real, but the wording of harm is not effective in community building. Naming the type of harm is critical, allowing us to navigate support as individuals experience and feel harm. Naming specifics is important. Harm is unique to the individuals and to the moment — it is always unique.

We are all capable of harm: – harming one another, and even ourselves. The philosopher Terence said, ys "*Homo sum, humani nihil a me alienum puto,*" meaning, "'*I am a human being. Nothing human can be alien to me*'." Any form of harm that has ever been caused by a human is something any of us can replicate: rape, physical violence, genocide, famine, all of it. Just because the ingredients exist within us in the form of unlimited possibilities does not mean that we must bake these ingredients into harm.

Allah is The One Who Harms and who has the ability to harm us in ways even we do not have the ingredients for. Yet, Allah does not. Allah can erase us and our entire bloodline from existence, yet doesn't. Allah can punish us in ways we can't even imagine, yet does not. The One Who Harms does not, yet as humans we are generous with our harm.

Within us exists every ingredient to humanity, which simultaneously includes the harm and the most beautiful of qualities. We have the privilege of choice in how we move in the world. If you choose harm, then you move away from The One Who Harms. And when we choose love and other ingredients, we move towards The Light.

57 Al-Hameed: The All Praiseworthy

My birth name has to do with praise — many of the prophets' names do. My maternal grandmother's family's name is Hamdan, which translates to "the ones who praise." Al-Hameed does not dictate that no one else is to be praised. It is knowledge and awareness that there is no praise without Al-Hameed.

There is nothing that we are capable of that is not Al'Hameed's. When I write a book, you should congratulate me and send me gifts, but ultimately, it is not my accomplishment alone. I have no achievements on my own. All of my accomplishments are an extension of my community and all by the will of Al-Hameed. I am only praiseworthy because Al-Hameed deemed it so. Everything beautiful I can ever bring forth is not mine.

Only Allah is The All Praiseworthy, for no one shares in the praise — it is not split amongst stakeholders. All Praise is for Al-Hameed.

41 Al-Haseeb: The Reckoner or Bringer of Judgement

There are two elements to Al-Haseeb, the first is an accounting of everything that ever has, could have, or will happen. The second is accountability.

I used to be — and still am in some ways — the historian of the family. For example, I keep track of who has hurt us and remember it forever. Forever lasts until accountability happens and will not be forgotten otherwise. I'm a pretty good historian, with a record spanning thirty of my thirty two years on this planet. But I know so little, and there is not much I can do to move anyone towards accountability. At the end of the day, all I can control are my actions. Everything beyond that is also beyond me.

Al-Haseeb is the Only One Who is The Reckoner and Bringer of Judgement. Only Al-Haseeb knows everything and is able to have universal accountability, at a level that we can't even comprehend within the intricacies of time and space. We can barely navigate a single conflict with a single community member. Al-Haseeb accounts for everything, in every life that has ever existed and will exist and moving us towards accountability.

Moving towards generative conflict and accountability is something that requires investment in one another and community — community that honors our shared purpose (stewarding the land and caring for one another). What would conflict look like if the judgement we considered is about stewarding the land and caring for one another? This is not impossible. However, it is something we must work towards. Al-Haseeb does not need to work towards it because is already The One who brings judgement upon us all and moves us towards accountability beyond even the best generative conflict and accountability practices.

27 As-Samee': The All Hearing

There's a saying that Al-Samee' hears what's in your heart. That has always been my connection with Al-Samee'. There were no interpretations concluding it was about something spoken out loud;, rather, it was usually the things that may never be uttered, — even from ourselves. Al-Samee' hears what is deep within our soul and everything else that we are already aware of. Often, the concept of hearing comes up with prayer. We pray to name yearnings. Al-Samee' hears those, hears past them knowing all that is to come and everything that has come.

What does it mean to hear for us as humans?

For me, in a lot of ways, hearing is about anticipating needs — not in a *I know better than you living your life* kind of way. Systems of oppression have not changed much over time, they recycle the same weapons again and again against us. Those of us doing the community work on the ground know how they will target us. By hearing what's in my soul, I can hear what's in yours. I am often asked what queer and trans Muslims need. I say everything — none of our needs are fulfilled. Someone who does not hear what queer and trans -Muslims need will go and try to conduct a five-year study to ask us again and again what we need, wasting five years of resources and not meeting any of our needs. The most impacted will always know best, and we do know best. We do not need immense amounts of labor to verify what we already know. When I say the most impacted, I am not referring to Muslims from upper-middle-class backgrounds, to cis people, to able-bodied people, or folks separate from displaced identity. I am referring to folks who have lived poverty, who have navigated immigration and/or carceral systems, who navigated displacement on a daily basis, folks who are told in every way that our death is irrelevant due to disability, race, or any of the many reasons (usually a mix and match situation).

When we hear one another, we are able to build infrastructure for care and stewardship. Humans are not that complex. Our needs are simple. What is complex is the messaging from systems of oppression telling us what we do and don't need when we have always known and named what our needs are.

28 Al-Baseer: The All Seeing

Outside of ableist culture, what does it mean to see? Less than three feet away from me, it is raining behind a thin layer of glass, water pelting off the concrete of sidewalks and asphalt of roads. Cars drive by, and individuals with and without umbrellas pass by. Puddles form erratically, some at corners of the intersection, others in the middle of the road. Suddenly, it gets brighter out, and the sun comes out, but the rain does not end, gifting blessings on this Christmas Eve.

These are things I see through my eyes, and if I close my eyes, take off my noise canceling headphones, I hear the rain above the coffee shop's music. I feel how it consistently pelts the ground — a different noise falling on the sidewalk vs. the road. Cars' sound different in the rain, walkers sound different, more erratic.

If I keep my eyes closed, do a quick body scan and allow myself to expand my conscious, I can see that the people sitting at the table next to me are struggling to find words to express their love for one another; I feel the person behind me anxious; I feel the barista wanting to not go home. If I keep my eyes closed and I send my consciousness downwards, I hear Xučyun, but I do not because sometimes I am scared of what she will tell me.

To see is not about the physical images that are captured through our eyes and processed by our minds. To see is to be with. To be with is to act with. Our lives are not a movie that we watch and separate ourselves from.

If I know someone is anxious, I have tools to support them. This is not to say that I will turn around and offer a therapy session to the person. In this case, it is being mindful of my own energy and instead giving the space calming energy instead of anxious energy that I myself could also be releasing. It could mean a smile. It could mean an extra tip for the barista. It could be a lot of things.

I am afraid of seeing land sometimes because I worry about whether or not I will truly be able to fulfill her demands at my current state. I am ungrounded, my mind is already pushing past its limits due to not doing my normal yoga, mediation, and writing practices that allows it to carry. My lungs have not been well in four months, their capacity to carry also impacted. If I take on more than what my bodymind can carry, my cognition, memory, and processing abilities will be impacted. For me that looks like no longer differentiating between time and space and no longer being able to keep track of where or when I am.

Seeing is a responsibility — many people choose not to see.

Al-Baseer is the All Seeing, seeing everything and always being with us. There is nothing missed. Al-Baseer does not see through eyeballs, Al-Baseer sees through everything in creation.

33 Al-Haleem The Forbearing One

There is a gentleness to Al-Haleem that humans can only aspire to. As we navigate the world around us, being forbearing requires an incredible level of emotional intelligence and non-attachment. To be forbearing requires moving within the anger, pain, and everything else that demands immediate responses from us. Anger is a beautiful emotion when used to take action and turned into creation. When we do not know what to do with our anger and pain, then we turn it inward, to ourselves or our community. To be forbearing is not to say that we are never angry. In fact, for us humans, it is through witnessing and honoring all our emotions that we reach a space of forbearance where we can be with them all.

Al-Haleem is The Forbearing One, perfectly balanced, always kind, always loving, always forgiving.

35 Al-Ghafoor: The All-Forgiving

It is said that there is nothing Allah loves more than forgiveness. In fact, if you combined all the forgiveness we are capable of as humans, it would only be a tiny fraction of the forgiveness Al-Ghafoor has. Humans are capable of such immense forgiveness, and it is still only a fraction.

In my work, I have seen survivors of rape, femicide, genocide, and other atrocities forgive their abusers. And it is just a fraction of what Al-Ghafoor does.

Al-Ghafoor contradicts the notion of a vengeful Allah, for if we can forgive one another, the possibilities of what that looks like for Al-Ghafoor are endless.

Many people would be shocked by what was previously mentioned, either because they don't have an example of human forgiveness, or because they themselves have not forgiven anyone.

Forgiveness is a choice, and Al-Ghafoor does not require that we forgive one another for oppression.

When I started one-on-one mental health peer support work, I was adamant that I would never work with individuals who had perpetrated sexual violence against children. This was due to sexual assault I experienced in my childhood. Within two years, I exclusively wanted to work with people who had. At the time, it wasn't that I had forgiven my abuser — I wanted to support people so that it never happens again. I have always been restorative and transformative justice oriented, and this was the work I yearned to do. It wasn't this experience that moved me towards forgiveness, for I know how to work with people without my ego being present.

I moved towards forgiveness eventually because I honored that, within me, there is a forgiving soul. I like to pretend otherwise sometimes, but I have forgiven everything and everyone. I may still remember, and I may not be the one to go out of my way to notify the other party that I have forgiven them, but if they show up, if they do the smallest of things, I will move on. I sadly smile writing this part because, in a lot of ways, we view forgiveness as weakness, as naivete. But if I know you will hurt me anyways, that doesn't necessarily change things. At the end of the day, I know how to care for myself post any harm. Your harm does not define me, but how I show up does.

Al-Ghafoor doesn't have to forgive us — doesn't need anything in exchange. When we stop viewing forgiveness as a form of exchange, we move towards Al-Ghafoor, and inevitably towards ourselves.

82 Al-Afu: The Forgiver

I was asked at an event — not for the first time — about the concept of intentional communities. The question specifically stated that most queer people wanted to move together, but we rarely did it. I have yearned for the same thing, and then people remind me that I do not like people like that. It's true, but there are a few I would move to 100 acres of land with. I'd co-live with them and the land. I say the reason that many of us do not take the risk is because we are terrified of the harm that we can cause one another. We are more afraid of one another than we will ever be of the state. I say a part of this is that we expect safety from one another, something none of us can guarantee.

No human can give you safety. We will harm one another. We will make one another feel uncomfortable. We will disagree. We will be triggered.

We will be disappointed. We will have conflict. All of those things are human. These are the things that light stars along our paths to show us where we are meant to grow. They are our constellations of guidance for truly liberatory communities. And like many of us, we might not look up as the stars are lit all around us. Without a recognition that we are human and to be human is all the things above and is to be compassionate and forgiving then we can't build intentional communities that move us towards collective liberation. Fear will prevent us from trying, and when it doesn't, and we commit to it, we will often fall apart because we are not prepared to be human with one another.

The Forgiver recognizes we are human, that we will not be perfect, that we adjust and adapt and grow. The Forgiver welcomes us back through forgiveness. Within the Islam that raised me, I was taught there are two types of harm, one to the divine and one to the divine's creation. The harm against the divine is forgivable only by The Forgiver. The harm against creation is only forgivable by creation. I found solace in this, withholding forgiveness to extend punishment to those who had harmed me in the afterlife. That rage was valid. The wounds festered, and they swelled as they were meant to and then tore apart. When I first started doing peer support, I said out loud that I would never work with abusers, particularly sexual assault abusers. In the years that followed, I found myself moving towards working with abusers almost exclusively, adopting a transformative justice philosophy in everything I do. Now, I believe everyone is worthy of forgiveness, and everyone is capable of accountability. That might be harder some days than others, but it is in not forgiving that I find more stars to guide my growth. At the end of the day, only Allah is The Forgiver, but by forgiving, I move towards wholeness.

Years ago, I reflected on the Arabic word for gratitude, and how it was rooted in forgiveness and wellness. Forgiveness moves us to wellness. I am grateful for every harm, no matter how small or large. I grow through them all. They do not define me — my community defines me, but they are lights on my journey for where I am meant to go.

36 Ash-Shakoor: The Most Grateful

During the eclipse in May 2023, I was at an inner dance retreat and reflected on gratitude, writing the following poem:

Gratitude
is inseparable from
forgiveness

in Arabic
"you're welcome"
meaning forgiving
a releasing or acquaintance
of guilt and pain

I forgive through gratitude, you
forgive through ...

Forgiveness عفو
is also rooted in عافية
healing,
wellness, whatever
inadequate english words to say:
gratitude is
forgiveness is
healing is
wellness is
wholeness is
me

Gratitude is about forgiveness and wellness. When we say Al-Shakoor is The Most Grateful, it is a statement about forgiveness and offering wellness to us all. Al-Shakoor doesn't need anything from us in return. The names of Allah that center core practices and pathways in our lives are for us to know how to live our lives. A life filled with gratitude is a life where we are not carrying all the bad that has ever happened to us. We are instead moving towards wellness.

This project is a great example of that. I did the 99 name of Allah countdown to spring 9 years ago. At the time, I was supporting an organization run by one of the worst humans I have ever come across. The project back then served as a lifeline months before Trump was elected, and before my PTSD would be retriggered. Those were some of the worst years of my life between 2015-2018, and I am grateful for all of it.

I am grateful because I still, nine years later, move towards Allah. Nine years later, something in me knew I would need these reflections again. I have been meaning to come back to this project for years, but it is only this year, immediately following the one year anniversary of Oct 7th, 2023, and after community violence had ravaged our communities, I return to writing this. I write this in a mental place that would not be considered well by many people feeling more disconnected from the community than I have in years. I am grateful for the disconnection. I am grateful to be here.

I told a friend recently that I enjoy being in this *I hate everyone* space because it has allowed me to step back into my needs so I can fully show up for community again. Nothing is wasted, and when nothing is wasted there is endless gratitude. I don't believe in waste — and this is a practice that I am not fully perfect at. The names of Allah show us the paths to move towards Al-Shakoor.

18 Ar-Razaqq: The All Provider

I was taught at the youngest of ages that Rizq (Provision) is provided from Ar-Razaqq and from Ar-Razaqq alone. I was taught this by both parents, but particularly by my mom who would manage to whip up an entire feast everyday after school to feed at least three families visiting us. Our house — barely a two-bedroom apartment for a family of eight — was filled with at least 20 people every afternoon. We were on food stamps, barely getting by, but we always had enough for the community. Mama taught us (I'm paraphrasing) that it's not about material wealth. That's easy. It was how you show up for the community.

I attempt to live my life with those same values because what's the point otherwise? What's the point in living life pretending that I am the one in control of resources and everything else that comes with it? Patriarchy has taught us what happens when we pretend that any group of people can be *The Providers*. Only Ar-Razaqq is The Provider. How things will come to us is not something we control. Within my work, I witness people who have $20 left in their bank accounts give that $20 to others, while individuals with half a million in savings (yes I'm including retirement) will expect a lot of "thank yous" for donating $20.

Abundance is a gift from Ar-Razaqq, while scarcity is a gift from capitalism.

Chapter 3: Divine Values

Art by Yaffa AS

85 Dhul-Jallal Wal-Ikram: The Lord of Majesty and Generosity

I get goosebumps writing this section. I am sitting at a random cafe in Oslo, a group of fabulous Sudanese Muslims sitting next to me.

I was asked a couple of days ago what my favorite name of Allah is these days, and I said Dhul-Jallal Wal-Ikram (The One of Majesty and Generosity). I adore this name for so many reasons. I adore that it is two names in one. I adore Majesty and Generosity, and I am humbled by the power of the names being inseparable. The name dictates that you are not majestic if you are not generous, and that generosity is majestic. In a world where the rich elite (a minority from a minority) rule by hoarding and extracting, leading to global catastrophe in every single possible way, this name is a challenge to all forms of oppression. Saying to billionaires and the world's elite: you are not Majestic, for you are not Generous. You may hoard, you may oppress, but you will never have true power, for only Allah is the Lord of Majesty and Generosity. And you are nothing.

Generosity is not charity. Generosity is not resource redistribution. Generosity is not reparations. Generosity and majesty exist beyond oppression. Everything listed above are oppression-driven systems, not generosity and majesty. Charity is to give what is yours supposedly. Resource redistribution is to recognize that what you have is due to the oppression of others, and you attempt to right a wrong. Reparations is trying to provide resources to account for a harm that was inflicted. All of them are based on oppressive systems in the current context we normally talk about.

Generosity and majesty on the other hand is how we are within the community, how we show up beyond oppression. Generosity and majesty intersect with community care, within and beyond oppression. Community care against oppressive systems is about surviving those systems; community care beyond systems of oppression is about fulfilling our purpose to steward the land and care for one another.

Even if the world's billionaires were to give away every penny that they have extracted from marginalized communities they will never be generous, nor will they be majestic.

Generosity is in taking what is yours, what has been given to us in our inherent power and gifts, and then utilizing that within the community for our purpose (stewarding the land and caring for one another) in this world and following The Right Path (Ar-Rashid). Inherent power is our love, compassion, thoughtfulness, wonder, imagination, creativity, and so much more that makes us human. Generosity is not a financial exchange because financial exchanges do not define humanity. Resources come and go, but in the best and worst of times, inherent power always exists, even when systems of oppression claim otherwise.

We are generous in how we show up for one another. We are majestic when we are truly fulfilling this purpose, where we recognize that everyone in the room is majestic.

I go back to a memory often from five or six years ago. I was talking to my then 14ish year old sister, who struggled with how she was showing up, fearful of her light. She was worried of coming off arrogant by accepting her gifts and abilities. I told her to claim herself as if she were royalty, and as if everyone else was too — also, the problem with royalty was that only some can be royal. She told me what I had told my mom years ago when she would remind me of similar things, "okay, sure." She's brought this moment up a few times since. I hope she and everyone else claim their light and learn that claiming our light does not diminish anyone else's. As a Leo, I know my light does not diminish anyone else's. In fact, when I am all that I am, I amplify everyone else's light too.

95 Al-Badee': The Initiator, The Originator, or The Incomparable

I say and write many things. I have most of my life, even during bouts of selective mutism. Yet, nothing I have ever said is original. I do not believe that I have ever had an original thought.

By the time I was born, countless generations of ancestors had come before. By the time I could comprehend words, folks around me were saying things they learned from their own or other peoples' ancestors.

By the time I was born, my blood cells and muscle tissue already had knowledge from countless others and from the land that birthed them.

By the time I was born, June Jordan, Audre Lorde, James Baldwin, Maya Angelou, and countless others had already published hundreds of books telling us how to move. The Quran had existed for 1500 years, countless other scriptures existed prior. In the Islam of my childhood, I was taught that Islam had always been the spiritual path from the first human on. Over time it was co-opted and weaponized, so Allah sent more messengers and prophets, again and again. With the co-option and weaponization we see all around us, it's easy to see this happening around the world.

Only Allah is Original, only Allah truly creates.

I am often called a prolific writer. The last twelve months before writing this, I wrote 9 books. The truth is that everything in them is recycled from ancestors, people around me, other brilliant thinkers, and most importantly Spirit. This recognition makes it easier to move through "creating," – or more accurately, in my opinion, "recycling."

The concept of ownership comes up again and again within the 99 names of Allah. Again and again, it is incredibly clear that we – humans — own nothing. There is a reason that so much of supremacist culture is about ownership, ownership of humans, of land, of resources, of wealth.

Moving beyond the concept of that I can originate something, and bring something brand new into the world makes it easier to move towards collectivism. I am of my community, my community built all that I am, all I invest back is already of the community. Collectively we build one another. Only Allah creates alone — only Allah creates.

75 Ath-Thaher: The Visible/The Manifest

The word Thaher comes from the root Thahar (ظهر), which is the action of becoming visible. It is a complete action, as in fully visible, not partially. I am grateful for the random instances when I have learned about other spiritual practices, and I find it fascinating that the feeling of the Divine is so similar. While doing an intensive yoga teacher training at an Ayurveda class, the teacher in Rishikesh India recited Surah Al-Ikhlas but he wasn't reciting it. He was just explaining what Samadhi is, which is the highest level of enlightenment and bliss in yoga practice. Indigenous practice looks so similar, including the art, the words, and the movements.

On a trip to Inis Mor, an Island in Éire, I was struck by ancient Irish embroidery that looked exactly like Palestinian embroidery. On my trip to Palestine in 2024, I learned that many of our Indigenous symbols look almost identical to those of some indigenous tribes of Turtle Island.

Allah is The Visible when we are willing to see.

In most practices, we train the body to be able to hold the divine. This is why prayer is a physical practice. We do not pray to connect through prayer. We pray to train our bodies to cultivate an ability to hold the Divine. When we train our bodies, we are able to see what has always been around us.

39 Al-Hafeez: The Preserver

When I lived in Ireland, on another trip to Inis Mor, I saw ancient Irish embroidery on fabrics. The embroidery looked nearly identical to Palestinian embroidery (tatreez). On my trip to Palestine (first and only in August 2024), I bought a rug from Gaza that has the original Indigenous Palestinian symbol — the symbols looked exactly like the ones Indigenous to Turtle Island. Across thousands of miles, before planes, phones, or whatever else we refer to as modern, our people have always been connected, and so much of it is still preserved.

So many have tried erasing so many of us, including entire races and genders. Yet, we have always existed and will always exist. Currently, we're seeing a new wave of trans-hatred and trans-erasure, but we will not go anywhere unless Al-Hafeez wills it. Trans people have always existed — you misgendering me doesn't change that. Experimenting on trans bodies is what led to an understanding of puberty and reproduction, yet supposedly we are a new fad. But we will always be here and have always been here. We will only stop existing when Al-Hafeez wills it.

So many of us are denied our existence, but no one can actually deny us — for they do not have the power. We are undeniable.

So many things remain preserved from thousands of years if we're looking for them. These 99 names of Allah have shown up time and time again, millennia before Prophet Mohammad for the first time. As a Muslim, I believe that all spirituality was one and the same at one point. Over time, spirit was hijacked and moved away from Al-Hafeez to serve human power and influence. We have seen this with every spiritual practice. But they are all one and the same originally. Allah is still Allah and did not begin existing 1500 years ago.

Al-Hafeez preserves everything. Nothing is lost. Some are visible, and some are not. If Al-Hafeez wills it, what is meant to be preserved will be no matter how hard anyone tries — and try they have.

11 Al-Mutakabir: The Majestic

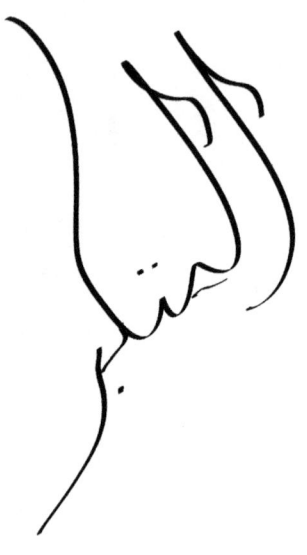

A redwood has majesty because Al-Mutakabir created it. I have majesty because Al-Mutakabir created me.

I would hear the word mutakabir as a child and it always came with a negative connotation. When a human is mutakabir, that generally means they have a big ego and make themselves bigger than they are. When our sense of who we are comes from our ego, either an expanded or deflated one, we tend to create our personhood through competition with others. An individualistic ego needs someone beneath them. A collectivist ego, which is defined through community, is able to honor that majesty comes from Al-Mutakabir. And what makes me magical is also within you.

When we view ourselves as magical because of who created us, then we view everyone in creation as magical. Some people choose to move away from their magic, and that is a choice, but Al-Mutakabir is still the one who created them.

Only Al-Mutakabir is majestic. Period. Al-Mutakabir is not majestic because Al-Mutakabir created us. Al-Mutakabir is the start and end of majesty. Nothing can compare, and nothing else is majestic on its own.

105 Aalam Alghayb Wal-Shahada: The Knower of The Unseen and The Witnessed

I'm scared of spirits. I don't say it often or speak about seeing and hearing what many cannot since years of mental health crises prevent me from sharing what is often stigmatized. I was scared of the dark until I was 10. I never got over that fear. I instead dissociated and forgot my fear. I am not scared of being harmed by spirits. I am scared of being seen and witnessed by them.

I do not fear punishment from Aalam Alghayb Wal-Shahada — I don't believe in a God that enjoys punishing creation. I love every part of who I am, and yet, I am still scared of being seen and witnessed because whenever I have been seen and witnessed in my life, it was when I have endured the most violence. Violence, as we define it as humans, doesn't happen in the dark and shadows. It is genocide on our social media feeds at 9 AM (all around the world and every day).

I started running from home when I was two — as soon as I learned to walk. I don't have an answer as to why I started running. I felt called to be elsewhere, so I saw an open door and left. As I got older, I hid in closets (physical and not metaphorical queer ones). I hid whenever anything went wrong. I hid every time I or anyone around me made a mistake. I could not tell you why back then, and I still can't tell you why now. I have only ever felt safe in the shadows, where I am unseen and not witnessed.

Years ago, when I first started camping (AKA living in a tent for 18 months due to homelessness), Mama would worry that I may not be safe in forests and deserts. Over the 18 months, I constantly told her that it is not nature that is to be feared — it is humans. She got there eventually. Now, she asks me if I am around people to gauge my safety.

I am not scared of Aalam Alghayb Wal-Shahada because I fear punishment. I fear not being able to lie and make things seem better than they are. I fear that spirits around me will know that I am the one who is not okay. Every day I smile and I show up, again and again. I'm honest about it, but it is rare for people to truly see me. In my one-person play *Harvesting Olives,* created with support from Rad Pereira, I allow an audience to witness me in my living room and kitchen. That is the closest people get to seeing me. No family, no families, no close friends have ever truly seen me.

Aalam Alghayb Wal-Shahada sees me every moment of every day. I may fear spirits but not being seen and witnessed by Aalam Alghayb Wal-Shahada. I am in reciprocal relationships with spirits. I give and they take, and I take and they give — it is like breathing. Aalam Alghayb Wal-Shahada needs nothing from me. I don't have to pretend to be okay to be in service because Aalam Alghayb Wal-Shahada doesn't need me to be okay at all times and to pretend one way or another. It is liberating to be seen, to not have to hide any parts of the realities of life right now. I have felt seen and witnessed by

Aalam Alghayb Wal-Shahada, and I am imbued with endless gratitude.

13 Al-Baari: The Maker

When I write a book, develop a curriculum, or create a piece of visual art, I am taking bits and pieces of things I have seen my entire life and things that may belong to ancestors, land, or a million other possible places. Nothing I "create" is unique or completely new — none of your favorite "creators" have created anything new. We all recycle different things, a reminder that "creation" in the human sense is always a collaborative process, even when working alone.

Al-Baari is The Only Original Maker, The Only Original Creator. Al-Baari creates from nothing — there is no influence, no recycling or upcycling, or anything else. Al-Baari creates uniquely in a way that we can never mimic, and in my opinion should never try.

I love that writing this book on my own in my apartment, or wherever I am, means that there are always countless others in these pages. Sometimes, that's actual collaboration, and mostly, it means that there are countless entities I do and don't know that are here writing this with me.

15 Al-Ghaffar: The Ever Forgiving

Al-Ghaffar and Al-Ghaffoor are similar names, with Al-Ghaffar being the exaggerated version of Al-Ghaffoor. Al-Ghaffoor is The All Forgiver, forgiving everything and wiping slates clean to move us towards accountability. Al-Ghaffar, the exaggerated version of The Every Forgiving, is a testament to the fact that Al-Ghaffar is in a constant state of forgiving. It is not just that Allah can forgive us, it is that Allah is constantly forgiving us. Every gift in our lives is an act of forgiveness. Every action is an act of forgiveness. Every breath is an act of forgiveness for us, for the planet, for everything in existence.

19 Al-Fattah: The Opener

One of my favorite verses in the Quran is verse 2:74:

ثُمَّ قَسَتْ قُلُوبُكُم مِّنۢ بَعْدِ ذَٰلِكَ فَهِيَ كَٱلْحِجَارَةِ أَوْ أَشَدُّ قَسْوَةً ۚ وَإِنَّ مِنَ ٱلْحِجَارَةِ لَمَا يَتَفَجَّرُ مِنْهُ ٱلْأَنْهَـٰرُ ۚ وَإِنَّ مِنْهَا لَمَا يَشَّقَّقُ فَيَخْرُجُ مِنْهُ ٱلْمَآءُ ۚ وَإِنَّ مِنْهَا لَمَا يَهْبِطُ مِنْ خَشْيَةِ ٱللَّهِ ۗ وَمَا ٱللَّهُ بِغَـٰفِلٍ عَمَّا تَعْمَلُونَ [2]

Even then your hearts became hardened like a rock or even harder, for some rocks gush rivers; others split, spilling water; while others are humbled in awe of Allah. And Allah is never unaware of what you do.

The visual of a hardened heart opening through three different paths is stunning — gushing open, slowly allowing water through, and crumbling by humility and awe. We live in communities within societies where genocide is debated. How much genocide, whose genocide, and by who doesn't matter — it is

---

[2] https://quran.com/en/al-baqarah/74

all debated. My people, my family, my life is debated everywhere. That last sentence is true as a Palestinian, as a trans person, as a disabled person. I can list out other identities, but you get the point. It's hard to witness and still believe that the hearts of the individuals saying pro-genocide and transphobic things can be opened, but they can be.

Al-Fattah can open any heart. Individuals who have done the worst actions can. It's hard to even write that individuals like Benjamin Netanyahu or Hillary Clinton could be redeemed. Al-Fattah opens their hearts and opens our hearts along the way.

I write that last paragraph with great difficulty, but I have seen it happen repeatedly. I have seen what happens when communities are faced with imminent threat (usually due to the climate catastrophe) and then come together. I have seen people send each other death threats but work together once all their houses are flooded or set on fire. Of course, it doesn't have to be after crises that hearts open, but they will usually open because of the crises. I believe people will unite when the climate catastrophe impacts everyone, except for the people who refuse of course. But why wait until then? Al-Fattah can open any heart at any time.

Chapter 4: Who is Allah?

Art by Yaffa AS

67 Al-Ahad: The One and Only One & 66 Al-Wahed: The One

قُلْ هُوَ ٱللَّهُ أَحَدٌ

Say, "He is Allah — One and Indivisible"

Surat Al-Ikhlas (Chapter 112) starts with the above words. Islam is monotheist, meaning that the belief in One God is integral in Islam. Throughout the Quran, Al-Ahad reminds us to not have belief in anything without Al-Ahad. The "without" part to me is critical to so many differences in practice across different sets, cultures, and individuals.

A few years ago, on a trip to visit family in Jordan, I found out that one of my sisters, who is a Cancer sun, married another Cancer sun. I knew they were having problems but did not know the details. I explained to her that I assumed their problems were related to their home, and that most likely their definitions of home are in contradiction to one another. My eldest sister immediately said astrology washaram. My response was simple, "so you're saying it's impossible that Allah created all these celestial bodies and gave us knowledge where we can use astrology as a tool to better fulfill our purpose?" I was right about the sister and her husband and, a year later, the older sister was talking about how Saturn transiting was impacting friends. There is nothing without Allah, and that doesn't mean that Al-Ahad has not gifted us all kinds of connection, knowledge, and understanding about ourselves, our purpose, and who Al-Ahad is.

Al-Ahad is The One and Only One, The Only Unique One there is no comparison, no competition, and no second, or third. It is not that there is Al-Ahad and then there are planets and stars. There is Al-Ahad, and Al-Ahad created everything in existence. Just like we have relationships with other humans, we are gifted the ability to have relationships with other forms of creation.

Al-Wahad is The One, The First of everything. Al-Wahad does not imply that there is a second and third to Allah, it is a reminder of the absoluteness of being The Number One, The Beginning of Everything.

92 An-Nafi: The Benefactor.

We know what is good for us. We really do.

I can't count the number of times that people will not come into my training or workshops saying afterwards that they're not ready, not ready to transform their relationships, jobs, etc. We know what is good for us. We know that liberation is good for us. We know The Light is good for us. We know so much of what is good, and yet, we turn away from it for something that is seemingly closer, more tangible.

The Benefactor is always providing us with everything good; it is a steady stream that never goes away. We turn away from this stream and yet it still finds us, again and again. Everything around us is a gift. Everything around us is meant to move us towards The Right Path – towards liberation. The streams exist whether or not we are aware of them. The streams exist whether or not we turn our backs on them, they will never go away.

A lot of religious language within white supremacist capitalism uses the language of punishment, abandonment, and withdrawal when discussing Higher Power. Allah is not making decisions as you are. Allah is not modifying The Light. Allah is not doing anything that is not constant and will be constant forever, pre and post the existence of all time. Allah is.

In Surah Al-Ikhlas Allah says:

Say He is One
Allah is The Eternal Refuge
He has never birthed Nor was He ever birthed
And there has never been nor will there ever be anyone equal

Allah is constant. There is no withdrawal. There is no abandonment. There is no punishment in the here and now. When we move away from The Benefactor it feels as if we have been abandoned and punished, as if the entire universe has withdrawn from us. But we are the ones who withdrew, and we are the ones who are able to move back towards The Light that exists regardless of anything we do or not.

48 Al-Wadood: The Loving/Kind One

I often say I am kind, not nice. Kindness comes from deep within us; it is a state of being. Kindness is a mix of compassion, grace, and love. Kindness does not always look beautiful to some individuals. For when we are kind, we are honest and might make people uncomfortable with the truth. Kindness is to offer feedback and support as we are all growing and moving towards Al-Wadood. Niceness is an obligation, and in many ways, it is more about the giver than the receiver — a way to feed the ego, and it's not necessarily about supporting other people. To be kind is to be connected. To be nice is to avoid vulnerability through deflection and lack of accountability.

These last few years I have had to have far too many difficult conversations that make everyone uncomfortable, and it is tiring. But it is kind. I could be nice and pretend like nothing is wrong, but vulnerability and naming values' misalignment is kind. Nice does not move us towards collective liberation.

Al-Wadood is The Kind One, not The Nice One — although Allah can be all the things. Al-Wadood's love is kind; it offers safety and wellness. It is truthful and vulnerable and does not hide what is seen as "ugly," according to societal standards. As we move towards Al-Wadood, we confront every part of our being: every value, every action, everything. We are born so close to Al-Wadood, and as we age, we move farther and farther away. To move back, we must transform every aspect of our lives, including moving away from the idea that we must be nice instead of kind. We move towards Al-Wadood by being kind to one another. We cannot move towards Allah without fulfilling our purposes: stewarding the land and caring for one another.

100 Al-Maajid: The Glorious, The Illustrious

Maajid comes from the Arabic root Majd (مَجْد), which can be translated to glory.

What does it mean to be glorious? Is there any glory outside of the ego?

Within our current societies, both within and outside of religion, we affiliate glory with warfare. Even in stories of the history of Islam and the Islamic Empire, glory is often found in war. But that hasn't always been the case.

For generations glory was about caring for others and stewarding land. Being trustworthy was the greatest honor. My great-grandfather was known as Al-Ameen in Yaffa, The Trustworthy. People left their belongings with him for safekeeping and he was glorious.

Allah's names are split into Al-Jalaal (The Majesty) and Al-Jamal (The Beautiful) in many interpretations. Al-Maajid is a name that encompasses Al-Jalaal, which is often seen as The Powerful, The Punisher. While Al-Jamaal is seen as having positive qualities. But I don't think Al-Jalal is about power in the ways that we have oppressively defined it. I don't believe glory is about war. I believe Al-Maajid is what happens when you're vulnerable. It is what happens when you are trusted. It is what happens when you have lived a life in service to stewarding land and taking care of the community.

Glory is not in committing genocide. Glory is not even necessarily found in steadfast armed resistance against oppression. The latter is a reality that none of us wish for but is necessary at times to overthrow systems. Glory is every day. Glory is in claiming non-capitalist and non-white-supremacist forms of success.

49 Al-Majeed: The All Glorious

Majeed is the exaggerated version of Majid, both sharing the same root. Al-Majid is The Glorious, whereas Al-Majeed is The All Glorious. All Glory is for Al-Majeed. For me, Al-Majeed elevates Al-Majid and extends it outwards, as if saying that there is no Glory without Al-Majeed. It is Al-Majeed that bestows glory upon anyone. We are never glorious without Al-Majeed.

68 As-Samad: The Everlasting/ The Eternal

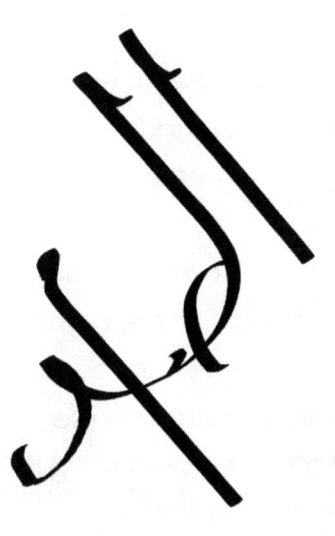

What does it mean to be remembered?

In some cultures, we fully disappear when we are forgotten after death. In others, we are always whole. I say I yearn to be forgotten, and, in fact, a lot of times I do. I have prayed in the past to be erased from existence — family and loved ones never losing anything at all, and I get to move on. I say I don't care if any of my work is remembered, and I don't.

But sometimes I care if I am erased. Erasure is violent, while forgetting is human. At the end of the day, I don't control either outcome. For all I know, I could be elevated as a prophet, or worse, as a God after my death, or even during my life. Someday, eventually, I will be forgotten — even if I am assumed to be a God. No one but Allah is Everlasting; we all fade with time. Both our actual selves and the fictitious selves that are erected postmortem.

Allah is The Only thing that is Eternal and Everlasting. Across hundreds of thousands of years, some humans will always remember, even as we forget ancestors and names for plants and animals, as empires rise and fall. All Empires fall, but Allah is The Everlasting. In many ways, we are currently at the end of the Empire. Every Empire has believed it is the one to withstand all time. They all die in the end. We all die in the end. What we leave behind is not ours to determine — it is not ours to carry.

May all we leave behind moving our communities towards collective liberation.

96 Al-Baqi: The One Who Remains

What is left when we physically die? What is left when this planet physically dies? What is left when the universe physically dies?

I am a death worker. I support people and communities as their bodies die. I support returning bodies to the land. I support families to understand that grief is not an absence, not an abyss. Grief is a solid part of who we are.

In my work, I find that so many people spend decades of time and energy trying to figure out the answers to the questions above, so preoccupied with understanding what is not meant for us to know. We cannot even comprehend the basic things around us, yet we yearn to understand what is endlessly more complex. There is so much we experience and feel, but until we have reached enlightenment and become one with Allah, it is as if we're trying to make sense of something that's locked behind several safes, and we're just pretending to be able to discern what is behind the safes.

What we do know is that Allah is still there beyond all death. When there is nothing left of us, Allah is still there. Many of us, regardless of spiritual practice, make so much of the world about us: Allah is about us; The Right Path is about us; Spirit is about us. Allah is Allah. We do not define Allah. We do not define The Right Path. We do not define Spirit. Allah is everlasting and will be here whether or not we are. As much as we destroy, we are still irrelevant. Perhaps we destroy to try to be relevant (think Napoleon). But we are not. We are here and then we are not. Allah remains.

12 Al-Khaliq: The Creator

Everything in creation that we do or don't know was and is created by Al-Khaliq. Every single tree, every leaf, every human, every cell within our bodies, every ounce of sea foam.

Everything.

As I write this, someone asks me if I'm here for the wedding. There is a party somewhere deeper in the redwoods, where EDM is being blasted, and I say maybe it's towards there. In the middle of this forest, there is an EDM party, a wedding, a writer on a bench, and countless others going about their day. And they may never encounter one another. I heard the music, but now I know there is also a moment of love here as well — it could be the wedding or countless other things. All of it is created by Al-Khaliq.

What happens to my resentment when I realize that the person who harmed me most is also created by Al-Khaliq? Some might look at that as blaming Al-Khaliq for that individual's actions — I look at it as a way to witness divinity even amid harm. This doesn't mean I keep this person in my life or even talk to them ever again, but I can recognize the sacred in that person, just like I can witness it in the leaves all around me and the redwoods shooting into the sky above, where it would hurt my neck to look for long. When I forget who I am, I remember through everything else in creation. I see all the possibilities. I could be evil, but here I sit within redwoods, choosing not to be. These redwoods — majestic and magnificent and calm and grounded — are made of the same particles as I am and all of us are made by Al-Khaliq. I can never be alone when I am connected to everything.

37 Al-Aliyy: The High

Al-Aliyy is The High. To say Al-Aliyy is The High is not to imply that there is anyone else a little less high. Al-Aliyy is the entire spectrum, and there is nothing in existence on that same spectrum. Al-Aliyy is a name connected to Al-Mutaali and Al-Jaleel. Al-Mutaali is a more magnified version of Al-Aliyy, while Al-Jaleel is saying Allah is The Most High, which also means The Most Honourable.

I think about competition sometimes. In most aspects of my life, I am not competitive. It is primarily due to a childhood where my parents compared me to others often, especially to a younger sister who needed to be the best. In the world I grew up in, there was a lot of competition, and early on, I knew that I couldn't compete — I wasn't on their level. People hear this and might think that I'm being disparaging. I am honouring that I am unique in the ways I am. I am not traditionally much of anything. I have learned to survive in this world, but a world filled with systems of oppression is not my world. I learned that I was in my own competition — no one to compete with, not even myself. People say that you should compete against yourself, but honestly, that doesn't make sense to my autistic mind. There are so many parts of me, but they're not in competition with one another, nor do they lose and win above one another.

In the world I choose to live in, we're all on our own spectrum; there are no valid or needed comparisons. We exist, and we're unique. If you're a great person, you're not great in comparison to someone else's standard. If you're a shit person, you're a shit person — period — but not compared to other awful people. I write books and create visual art, and I refused to compare my own work to one another. Things are just the way they are, nothing is higher than another, no one is higher than another. Only Al-Aliyy is The High, and we're not in the competition at all.

38 Al-Kabeer: The Most Great

While traveling in Falasteen, we had an idea to put speaker collars around stray cats and have them blast "Allahu Akbar" at random times — "the zionists would be gone in days," we would laugh. Allahu Akbar means Allah is Greater, and that terrifies oppressive people. When we say Allahu Akbar, it is a promise that nothing is lost or wasted, and everything is honored within our lives, or the next, or when we are all called to accountability.

I don't have a lot to say here — everything I have said is to say, Al-Kabeer is The Most Great. Period.

65 Al-Waajid: The Finder

What does it mean to be found? I think about the times when I was truly seen, and the times when I was not seen at all. I remember my second-grade teacher telling me I can do something everyone else said I was bound to fail at. I remember fevers, bee bites, and broken bones that are visible and yet not seen.

To see is not a function of the eyes. It is about witnessing the gifts around, within, and beyond us. There is nothing in the universe that is lost to Allah, for Allah is The Beginning and The End, The First and The Last, and everything is Allah's creation.

To say Allah is The Finder is not to say that Allah has lost anything. It is saying that Allah — unlike us — is always witnessing. We are always seen. We were created seen, and we die seen. We are witnessed at every stage of our existence. We are seen as beings made of land descendants of stars, holding memories of our ancestors. Allah sees all of it. Allah Finds all that we are. And as we move towards Allah, we move towards our answers.

Chapter 5: Collectivism

Art by Yaffa AS

52 Al-Haqq: The Truth

Perhaps in other ages, there wouldn't be such a divide about what is true. There are some incredible resources out there about being able to gauge the truth, such as Seema Yasmin's book, *What The Fact?* But largely, most people don't know how to move through knowledge and identify the truth. Even when we do, we still get it wrong sometimes. I see this in my work often.

Working in dozens of countries, I might get information from one person that contradicts information from one of their neighbors. It's not that one is lying, and the other is truthful. It's that life is complex, and so are our experiences in life. Most people can't navigate feelings from actions. This isn't to say the truth is not important. Our ability to move through truth is instrumental to moving towards collective liberation. But we'll never fully be there.

Al-Haqq is The Truth, knows the full truth, knows every detail of every event. We will never be able to hold 100% of everything all at the same time. That's why accountability partners and transformative justice work is integral to moving towards liberation. Collectively, we move closer to The Truth. Alone, we will never be able to hold even a fraction of truth.

83 Ar-Rauf: The Ever Compassionate

The Arabic root for the word Rauf is ra'afa (رأفة), which means to have compassion and mercy.

Compassion is a buzzword that is overused in many spaces. Many have defined it over the years, and for years, a debate has raged on which is better: empathy or compassion. Some define empathy as an ability to connect with emotions, while compassion is showing up fully. Others define it the opposite way. In Arabic, Rauf is the exaggerated version of Ra'afa, an already active verb. I will not go into debates of what is and is not, I leave that to you to define things with your own communities — in the context of the 99 names of Allah, The Ever Compassionate is active, always active.

The Ever Compassionate is not only compassionate sometimes, The Ever Compassionate is in a constant state of compassion and having mercy upon us. This sounds contradictory to previous names, where we discussed that The Ever Compassionate does not interfere in our everyday realities, and instead allows us to practice free will and define our paths. To me, this is an acknowledgment that compassion is not in response to an event — it is everlasting and constant.

We are often taught to show more compassion to others during times of crises, rarely addressing that if we were to show compassion constantly we might not be in a state of crises as often.

The Ever Compassionate is always compassionate, not just when we pray and beg for mercy, but every moment of every day. Compassion is in the air we breathe, the trees that breathe in and out with us, and all our kin, human and nonhuman. Compassion is in the energy that moves between us. Compassion is in land that calls to us, prays with us, grieves with us, celebrates with us. Compassion is in stars that shine on us, moving us towards ways of being even as we deny them.

I wrote this while waiting in an airport. My flight from Stockholm to Barcelona got delayed (again!). On the way to Stockholm, a friend asked me what growth I yearned for. That took us on a journey into a conversation about how I wanted to be supported. As I write this, I recognize that I want compassion, constant compassion. I don't want soup just when I am sick, or someone to check in because of a status saying I'm not okay. I want soup at random times just because. I want neighbors to send me food, and I send them things, not in exchange, but because we are compassionate to one another. If we wait until things fall apart, we will not have capacity to truly be there for one another.

I say all this knowing that I no longer have it in me to be checking in on friends and family like I am used to. I no longer have the capacity to send care packages and messages. I am tired. I think most of us are tired as we respond to emergency after emergency. Over time, our care is depleted because it is in response to emergencies instead of constant, spread out, beyond a single crisis. Compassion is a natural state of being as a human, it is meant to be in every practice of our culture.

In oppressive cultures, we are hyper individualistic. Within individualistic societies, community care is seen as foreign and wrong. Collective societies, on the other hand, are built on community care. What will allow us to move from individualism to collectivism is community care.

40 Al-Muqeet: The All Nourisher/The All Sustainer

I have three plants in my house that I leave to be on their own quite often, and I am honestly shocked they are still alive. I water and take care of them when I am here, but leaving plants unwatered for two months at a time is a lot to ask of them. Yet, they survive. A lot in the world is undernourished, yet still sustained. The circumstances we live through are unlivable in so many ways, yet here we are, still here.

I have dealt with malnutrition, sleeping in freezing temperatures, and...you get the point. On paper, all of those things are some of the worst things, yet they were exactly what I needed in those moments in time. This isn't to fetishize trauma or to talk about growth through abuse — this is to say that in my unique life, within my unique circumstances, I needed those things to get to where I am today. I do not wish any of these things on anyone, nor will I ever believe these things could be good for you. I believe that Al-Muqeet always nourishes us, regardless of what circumstances look like from the outside.

Some might wonder how I can believe in that when so much of my life and work is about some of the worst things that humans have ever done to one another. As a person who honours death, I know that there are far worse things. I see them everyday. I don't have all the answers, but to me, what humans do to one another doesn't take away from Al-Muqeet being The All Nourisher.

44 Ar-Raqeeb: The Watchful One

We use the word Raqib when we talk about watching children or others who might need some caretaking. When you watch a child, you are attentive in a way that you might not be otherwise. It's not that you're constantly looking — it's a mix of awareness, prediction, and being ready to act as needed. In a lot of ways, being watchful is the same as the process for being strategic (read the strategy essay in *Whispers Beneath The Orange Grove*).

Ar-Raqeeb is The Watchful One, who is watching over all of us. Allah's awareness encompasses all knowledge and ways of being. Ar-Raqeeb is the Only One who can truly watch over us. Even in the most caring relationships, we miss so much of what's happening in each other's lives, even living together and spending every waking and sleeping moment together.

We miss a lot. I would know — my childhood was a childhood where everyone missed every form of violence I experienced. For a long time I think I resented the people around me at the time; I have multiple poems titled, *Weinkom (where were you?)* in a forthcoming poetry collection, *Sage to be published May 2025.*

Weinkom (where are you?)
writing a report
to send to yt
people who can not
understand it
I realize that I hold
anger, so much anger
towards My family
all of them, S, D, E,
L, A, Mama and
Baba, just not
the babies

Where were they?
when the pills found
my belly and didn't

*let go for 35ish
hours*

*Where were they?
when three hospitals
tossed me around
like an expired salad
burying the mold
no one wanted*

*Where were they?
when I was so cold
sleeping on a bench
dodging men trying
to rape me
my stomach empty
except for the air
I desperately wanted
to deny it*

*Where were they?
after every breakup
after the dozens of losses*

Where are they now?

*when we haven't
properly talked in
months, years even*

*in 40 houses
13 years, and 9
countries
no sister has ever visited
a home of mine
perhaps if they do
it'd no longer be home*

I searched for these three poems in three different collections, and I could not help myself from reading from one of the forthcoming collections, *Stygian*. My heart flutters, beating erratically despite not drinking any coffee today. I feel a warmth that I haven't felt in days, and I smile to myself in the midst of the crowded cafe, where moments earlier, I was only thinking of pain. Ar-Raqeeb is always watching out for us, always.

7 Al-Mu'min: The Grantor of Faith/The Grantor of Security

In Arabic, the word for faith and the word for safety are rooted in the same word Eman (إيمان). I believe language can be really powerful as a way of communicating common concepts, and as a way of preserving history. Since you can break down any Arabic word into a root, it means that for thousands of years as it developed communities created instruction manuals for life within every letter.

Due to my upbringing, I had lost a lot of connection with Arabic as a language. Although I speak fluently, I do not think of emotions and concepts in Arabic organically; as in I have to translate from english to arabic in my head. Yet, it is only when I move emotions and concepts to Arabic that I can truly grasp them.

I have never felt safe, not in the societal sense of using that word. Safety that is defined as being away from harm is something that has never existed for me. As I grew older, I also began to understand that harm is not something merely inflicted upon us — harm is impact from rough edges piercing one another regardless of intention. Harm is as much my domain as it is something others can do to me. Safety is not something anyone can guarantee, according to this definition.

When I bring up faith and safety into the same sphere, the conversation changes entirely. Instead of safety being a guarantee of no harm, safety becomes having faith in something where you know that no matter what harm is inflicted upon you, different entities got your back: Al-Mu'min, yourself, other people, stars.

I have rarely felt that other humans will have my back in any meaningful ways, not family, not friends, not co-organizers. But I have always felt safe in my belief in Al-Mu'min. I walk in a world that would love to kill, punish, or destroy me, yet I walk around as if they can't do anything to me at all. My sense of safety comes from a profound faith beyond anything that any human can do to me. This life is short. Your violence meaningless.

8 Al-Muhaymin: The Protector

He says my arms feel safe when I hold him. I squeeze tighter because I know what it feels like to never know safety. My first moment of consciousness is one of violence. The second, third, and so many others that followed filled voids with violence. I learned so early on that there is no safety, not in the day, not in the night, not in public, not in private.

As a child, the only safety I felt I had was in hiding or underneath my blanket, where it felt like no one could find me. This was triggered due to various reasons, mostly being an autistic child who experienced multiple forms of violence from my extended family.

Safety is rare, yet at the same time, the person who felt safe in my arms is not a longtime friend or partner.

This was our second time meeting, yet he felt safe. In a lot of ways, it's so easy to feel safe, but it's hard to find. The thing is no one can guarantee our safety. I didn't do anything special; he did all the work. He felt safe — I just existed in that moment.

Only Al-Muhaymin can truly protect us. I choose to believe that Al-Muhaymin is always protecting me and everything in existence. No human can protect us, and if they say they can, then they are promising something that's unachievable.

Only Al-Muhaymin can truly protect us. Many will take that as a statement about all the people who aren't being protected and view it as a failure for Al-Muhaymin. Al-Muhaymin is not reacting in every instance in our lives. I choose to believe that Al-Muhaymin is always protecting us across time and space and lives in ways that sometimes feel like we're not protected at all, but we know so little.

22 Al-Baasit The Expander/The Reliever & 21 Al-Qaabid The Restrainer

When I think of Al-Baasit and Al-Qaabid, I think of our hearts beating — how they contract and expand, allowing blood to flow through our bodies for everything within them to function. I think about lungs, expanding and deflating with every breath. I think about how trees mimic the same function in reverse. I think about how the Earth's lungs are targeted in The Congo.

In many ways, the concept of restraining or being restrained is seen as a negative, but everything is meant to exist in equilibrium. We inhale taking and exhale giving back. We are meant to be in harmony.

When we play one role alone, it usually does not end well. I think about this as someone whose primary role has been the caretaker for family, friends, and even strangers. I give a lot, and sometimes I find that there is no one who is able to reciprocate. It is not that people do not want to, but there aren't many people with the right skills to support someone like me, so I remain the caretaker.

When we give without reciprocation and are not careful enough, we end up developing resentments. Resentments are fine when we know how to move through them. When we do not, they fester and swell, impacting us emotionally, physically, and spiritually. Resentments are usually leftover anger that we haven't cleared. Anger lives in our liver. Depending on the type of resentment, it could impact our liver or develop into anxiety and low self-esteem, moving to our pancreas.

At my current state, as I write this, I have a stiff neck (both sides for the first time in years), a stomach that's welcoming ulcers, and breathing severely impacted due to lung scarring. These symptoms started months ago with my lungs, followed by a stiff neck on the right side, then stomach pain, and now finally the other side of my neck. Oh, and migraines!

Our lungs carry our grief. I lost my voice entirely on Oct 7th, 2024, the one year anniversary. Since then, my breathing has been impacted, and I know this means that what I am carrying is spilling over. As grief started spilling over, specifically due to community violence, it festered into anger. The liver is connected to the right side of our necks. My neck has been stiff on and off for three months while I'm writing this collection. The liver is also connected to our stomachs and part of our digestive system — yay ulcers. The pancreas impacts self-esteem and anxiety more broadly. Resentment turned inwards means questioning your own value. Am I the reason I was harmed? Am I unlovable?

We're not meant to just give without receiving anything in return. This is not human. Our role on this planet is to steward the land and to care for one another, neither of which can happen alone. This is not to say that those of us who have had to give a lot more are to blame. If everyone gave in the ways they needed to, we wouldn't have this problem.

Sometimes the problem is the caregivers, I explored this in the essay Letting Go in *Whispers Beneath The Orange Tree*. Often though, givers keep giving because there is no infrastructure to support us to be more balanced. This relationship becomes extractive, which leads to resentment.

Giving and taking is not as simple as me giving you a dollar and you taking it. Giving and taking is beyond human relationships. Your giving and your taking need to be in line with that. For example, if you work at Google and are making $200,000 a year — money made off of genocide — your contribution is different than someone making minimum wage at an anti-genocide business. I talk about this often, but in the first case I expect you to be buying people houses. For the latter, I still expect you to be buying people houses, but in a very different way. The first should be a financial contribution, the latter can be research, co-signing, fundraising for a downpayment. The possibilities are endless.

Unfortunately, most people view their role as survival — I'm talking about the person in tech making a quarter of a million dollars a year and thinks they're poor. The bar of what we do for and with one another is so low in individualistic societies that those of us with higher standards end up doing far too much because the majority are not meeting us there.

Allah is Al-Baasit, The Expander and Al-Qaabid, The Restrainer, offering a perfect balance. Allah expands our realities to be able to give and restrain aspects of our lives, so that we may learn to take and truly be in community. Only Al-Qaabid is beyond this balance, for Al-Baasit does not need anything in return.

31 Al-Lateef: The Gentle One

I wrote this in the morning after nearly 20 hours of excruciating abdominal pain. This is not the first time I have had ulcers, and despite everything I know to care for myself during this time, it was still excruciating. Between the ulcers and salmonella a few years ago, we've had a rough few years. My stomach and I have a tense relationship. It's also a longer history of being stabbed in nearly all my previous lives and the yearnings of a trans person who cannot carry a baby in this body. It's incredibly complicated. During times of this kind of pain, I know that the only answer is gentleness.

I know stress makes things worse. I know forcing myself up makes things worse. I know that there might be days when I have to stay lying down. I know on those days my migraines will intensify, and I have to pick which to care for. On those same days, my neck will stiffen. Painkillers will help with one and make others worse. I know doctors will question everything I tell them. and ultimately not listen, giving me the wrong medication and nearly killing me yet again.Salmonella was rough.

So I fast, the one thing I know will take it away and risk the potential binging that might follow making it all worse. The last time I was in pain for four months before Ramadan came along. My younger sister who also had ulcers ended up in excruciating pain when she tried fasting. I was the opposite. As soon as I started fasting the pain went away, even with eating suhoor and iftar. I ended the month without any of the ulcers I started with. This was the first year in probably half a dozen when I was able to fast the entire month.

Writing this reminds me of the one moment of gentleness from my mom as a child — my mom is great, and life is hard. I was six, we had just moved to Arizona, and it was Ramadan. Like many children, I wanted to fast as a child thinking it was the coolest thing. I still do. I woke up one day late for suhoor. It was probably seven; everyone was asleep except for

Mama. For some reason, I thought she'd yell at me for missing suhoor, but she wrapped me in a blanket instead and told me it was okay. She made me a laughing cow sandwich and smiled at me. Everything about that morning was gentle.

I imagine Al-Lateef as that moment spread out across every single moment of our lives, that smile constant and amplified by a number I can't even imagine. The gentleness Allah has for us is infinitely more than anything we can show one another.

That single moment of gentleness transformed my life. I can't even imagine what having access to gentleness consistently in life from other humans would amount to.

88 Al-Ghanii: The self-sufficient

We all need something. Most of us need lots of things. Even when we are materially satisfied, we still need to breathe. We need — that is what makes us human, that is what makes us alive. Even when we're dead, we still have needs, our bodies to be returned to the ground and honored and potentially more depending on what you believe happens to us when we die. To need is not bad. To want is not bad. To desire is not bad. All are natural.

Humans are communal beings. We literally will not survive on our own as babies, nor can we truly be on our own as adults entirely, not for too long anyway. Beyond individual needs, we are meant to be collectivist, not individualistic. Individualism leads to human decay and the death of all things as we currently witness in the climate crises. We are meant to be in community. The greatest threat to systems of oppression is community.

While meeting with a friend recently, they shared that they wanted to ask a question during my last event in Manchester, UK but did not want to take space. Their question was how do you know when you're in community. The question I often ask spaces is: who has your back, specifically if you can't pay rent who will pay your rent? It's not actually about rent. Rent is just an example of something linked to our survival on a surface level that can signal community. Community is a place where you are part of an ecosystem, almost as if we all breathe together. I have been collectivist my entire life. I am not well if those around me are not well. To the point of getting ill when one of my sisters would be sick. We know when we are in community when we have a shared purpose and know that none of us are disposable.

Unfortunately, very few people are in genuine community with other humans – even those of us doing community building work. But we do not have to be of a specific community to be collectivist and to move towards collective liberation. Community is a lot more than relationships with other humans. We are in relationship with the land, animals, plants, spirit, air surrounding us. They are also part of our community. We can always be moving towards collective liberation, even shunned from the communities we yearn for. Many people will give up on causes because of harm within the community. Collective liberation is not about certain individuals or even a single community. It is about the entire ecosystem of existence — it is about the reality that we are liberatory beings who need liberation to survive.

Only Allah is The Self-Sufficient. The rest of us are at the mercy of collective liberation.

Chapter 6: Purpose

Art by Yaffa AS

87 Al-Jamii: The Gatherer

Our survival is intertwined, with one another as humans and with every living being, including the planet we are tasked with stewarding. Yet, we find every reason to be divided. Systems of oppression divide us on a daily basis. Many of us work to build community spaces to mobilize community for collective liberation, but no matter how effective we are, we will never all gather and rally behind a single thing — it simply will not happen. Only Al-Jamii can fully gather us and that's okay.

There is a myth that states that we need everyone for the revolution, that unless everyone was on board for collective liberation, we would not get there. That can't be farther from the truth. During every crisis I have organized around, there are always people who will actively stand against collective liberation.

The work happens anyways, and they either come along eventually, or they are left behind.

There has never been a time when humans have been fully united when it comes to collective liberation. It is amazing what a few can do to influence the masses. The world we currently live in is the utopia of a select few. When a single person moves towards liberation, countless others follow, while countless others move away. The world is not only for humans — we are not the sole decision-makers, no matter how much we think we are. Even if every human did agree on something, it does not change the realities that exist beyond all of our control.

We cannot be the gatherers because we will never know what is in fact best for everything in existence. Only The Gatherer knows for certain. We can be intentional on our journeys as we move towards collective liberation, but how and when is beyond us.

86 Al-Muqsit: The One Who Is Just, The Equitable

In a lot of ways, justice is pretty basic, at least when we consider the levels of oppression we are entangled in day in and day out. But it's a little trickier when we dig a little deeper, just beneath the surface. Is justice different for an individual vs. a community vs. a system? Who defines justice? Who defines it today, tomorrow, the day after? Who has defined it in the last 500 years?

I work at the intersection of conflict and collective liberation. I can pretend to know what justice and what equity are from time to time. but in reality, I'm just as clueless as everyone else. And that's not a bad thing. I'm talking interpersonally here. I'm not talking about a question of genocide, femicide, famine, rape. I'm talking about walking into a room of loved ones and leaving a little more broken and wondering what comes out when there is nothing left. I'm talking about well-intentioned people who hurt you more than anyone ever has. I'm talking about you. I'm talking about me.

The answer is simple — it's The One Who is Just, The Equitable. But if every spiritual practice starts from the same starting point of divinity, then have they all defined it properly? We know this is not the case. If everyone who proclaims to define justice from divinity actually did, then our world would look very different. Justice in a community within immense systemic oppression is not perfect. If it was, we wouldn't need to dismantle these systems.

17 Al-Wahabb: The Giver of All

Although Al-Wahhab and Ar-Razaqq are similar in many ways, a large difference is that Wahabb is used for gifting. Al-Wahabb is The Giver of All, with everything given to us a gift, and nothing should be wasted. The word Wahabb can also translate to bestow upon implying that there is a responsibility in the gifts we are given.

I think of Wahabb in relation to mutual-aid in comparison to charity. Mutual aid is a responsibility — to receive and to take are both responsibilities. When you receive mutual-aid, you affirm your commitment to community and to the larger purpose we are here for. Receiving mutual-aid is not "*I paid my rent now*" — mutual aid is "*I paid my rent now, which frees up X capacity to support Y and Z in other areas.*" Mutual aid that ends with just an exchange is charity or resource redistribution.

Al-Wahabb has granted us everything in our lives, whatever we consider good or bad, and everything in between. All of it is a gift, there is no such thing as something not being a gift. That gift carries with it a price tag — stewarding land and caring for one another, **our purpose.**

25 Al-Muiz: The Giver of Honour

Every honour bestowed upon us comes from Al-Muiz, no matter how much we try to pretend it's elite institutions who honour us. Do institutions honour us? What is a Noble Peace Prize when it is given to people who have committed genocide? What is the value of an Oscar, a Grammy, or any other "prestigious" award when hundreds of millions are displaced due to genocide and the climate catastrophe?

When I say Al-Muiz is The Giver of Honour, I am talking about the only Honour that matters: being on The Right Path. Our greatest honour is the purpose bestowed upon us: to steward the land and care for one another.

Have you ever supported someone? I mean really supported them, not from a place of ego, but from a place of genuine connection and care. How did that feel?

When we align with our greatest purpose and move beyond our ego, every action feels like a drink of water after days without water. It is a sense of warmth that encompasses all that we are after a brutal winter. That is the honour that Al-Muiz bestows upon us. It is not an award to recognize our egos. It is a recognition that we are whole, regardless of what systems of oppression tell us is a great honour and what is not.

Capitalism tells us we must be rich to be successful. Other systems of oppression will tell us that it's titles and accolades. At the end of the day, none of them matter. In a collectively liberated world, what rich, cis-straight white men have deemed important will no longer be of value. What matters is whether or not we fulfill our purpose here: stewarding the land and caring for one another, the greatest honor, The Right Path.

97 Al-Warith: The Heir/The Successor

Al-Warith means "The Heir" or "The Successor." Within white supremacist capitalism, the concept of inheritance and succession is incredibly problematic. We inherit the land, houses, money, and other things when loved ones die (if we have generational wealth). We even inherit "rights" to children (do not argue with me about this, guardians have "ownership" over children in most places).

Inheritance is something that changed over time, varying drastically prior to Abrahamic religions. With the rise of Judaism and then Christianity, inheritance became a male-dominant concept with those deemed as non-male unable to inherit. In Islam, 1500 years ago, this concept was shifted in drastic and revolutionary ways, creating very specific laws of inheritance and caretaking based on those rights. For 1500 years in Islam women inherit, not as a possibility but as a requirement. The last 1500 years showed the opposite happening in many parts of the world, opposing the European society that centered every societal concept around men. Every concept can be and has been weaponized, this is not a statement about Islam inheritance laws being perfectly implemented.

The concept of inheritance is incomplete without an understanding of "ownership" and claiming a decolonized practice beyond it. We do not own land, thus we can not inherit land. What we inherit is caretaking and stewardship of land. Material resources are only to aid us in our paths to steward land and largely this planet. In the Quran, Allah refers to humans as Khalifas, stewards or caretakers of the land. Regardless of who is inheriting, the true inheritance remains the same. It is always about stewardship, not about expanding material wealth generationally like it is the norm today.

وَإِذْ قَالَ رَبُّكَ لِلْمَلَٰٓئِكَةِ إِنِّى جَاعِلٌ فِى ٱلْأَرْضِ خَلِيفَةً ۖ قَالُوٓا۟ أَتَجْعَلُ فِيهَا مَن يُفْسِدُ فِيهَا وَيَسْفِكُ ٱلدِّمَآءَ وَنَحْنُ نُسَبِّحُ بِحَمْدِكَ وَنُقَدِّسُ لَكَ ۖ قَالَ إِنِّىٓ أَعْلَمُ مَا لَا تَعْلَمُونَ

'Remember˺ when your Lord said to the angels, "I am going to place a successive ˹human˺ authority on earth." They asked ˹Allah˺, "Will You place in it someone who will spread corruption there and shed blood while we glorify Your praises and proclaim Your holiness?" Allah responded, "I know what you do not know."

Since this land is not ours, these resources are not ours. These bodies and minds are not ours. And everything belongs to Al-Warith. Allah, then, is the only Inheritor, the only Heir, The only Successor. Allah did not give us this world — Allah allows us to steward this world. We can never be heirs to something that can never and was never given to us.

The Right path is not ours to claim. The summit is not ours to colonize. Allah is not ours to claim ownership of. Everything that Allah has created is not ours to claim ownership of. Nothing belongs to us. It is in this absence of ownership that we can move towards the Right Path, move towards Allah. Ownership is an imbalance, imbalance moves us away from sabr, from patience.

24 Ar-Raafi: The Exalter & 23 Al-Khafid: The One Who Humbles

I am a Leo. Leos are often seen as arrogant and needing to be the center of the universe. In reality, Leos are like the sun — we exist, and people gravitate towards us. The difference between a Leo who has moved past their ego and one who has not is that when you have not moved past your ego, you believe that you are the center of the universe, and because you think you are, it means that everyone is beneath you. When you have moved past the ego, you recognize that you are the center of the universe, but so is everyone else.

I grew up in a world that constantly told non-white, non-cis, non-straight, non-rich people to make ourselves smaller so people can be comfortable around us. Even in relationships, I would make myself seem smaller. I would have to convince other people again and again that they are in fact worthy of being around me. But I don't believe that humility is about making yourself smaller for the sake of others' comfort. A truly humble person is someone who can honour all that they are and honour all everyone else is at the same time. My light does not diminish your light.

Allah does not need any of us to be smaller than we are. Al-Raafi created us as we are. Al-Khafid can take away the gifts that have been bestowed upon us. I find a sense of peace in between — we are what we are. We have a purpose: stewarding land and caring for one another. Very little matters to me outside of that.

45 Al-Mujeeb: The One Who Answers

I write this on Christmas Day — tired, burned out, and so close to returning to a world of suicidality (the only thing preventing me is I will not give these systems the benefit of a non-strategic death). I write this without anyone to call or turn to. It's not that people around me do not care, they do. It is that everyone around me is burned out from caretaking, and there is nothing left for me without them being harmed in the process. The caretakers are not okay. I am not okay.

I have never had anyone to turn to, usually holding it together long enough to see everyone else fall apart before me. In the midst of all of this, Al-Mujeeb (The One Who Answers) always finds me.

I see Al-Mujeeb in the top layer of chai swirling around my cup, creating rivers and smokeless flame. I see Al-Mujeeb in the smile of a child walking by. I see Al-Mujeeb at the obnoxiously loud table next to me. I see Al-Mujeeb in the pokemon game I play for no reason whatsoever on my phone. I see Al-Mujeeb in every word I write, eternally grateful that no matter how I feel, my fingers type away. And these words live on even if I don't.

I don't want anything from Al-Mujeeb as I write this, other than the best. Not the best that I or anyone in society defines, but the best as defined by Al-Mujeeb. I don't ask for people to show up for me. I don't ask for burnout to leave me. I ask for whatever is best. It's not just that Al-Mujeeb is The One Who Answers — Al-Mujeeb is The One Who Already Has Answered. Every part of my life is divinely inspired, sculpted in ways that inshaAllah always moves me towards Al-Mujeeb. Even today's feelings are a part of it. Writing this book is a part of it. Everything moves me. I aim to move as long as I am alive.

47 Al-Hakeem: The All Wise

Beyond knowledge, there is an entire realm of wisdom. It is the practice of knowledge, in kind and loving ways. Wisdom is generated through knowledge, whether we are aware of this knowledge or not. For example, we might have knowledge passed down to us through our bodies, energetics, spirit, or any other possibility. Not everyone will find wisdom beyond knowledge. Some people live at the point of knowledge, never wanting to take it beyond that. Sometimes, we're not called for wisdom, and that's okay.

Others will be able to work with knowledge and immediately move to wisdom, while others might take decades. All of that is okay. We are all on our individual journeys, and we all have a different role to play in fulfilling our purpose: stewarding the land and caretaking for one another. We are valid. What is not valid is when we are in a stage of our growth, and we believe that only we could be wise — that is unwise.

Al-Hakeem is not like us. Al-Hakeem does not move through knowledge to reach wisdom, for Allah is The All Wise (Al-Hakeem) and The All Knowing (Al-Aleem).

20 Al-Aleem: The All Knowing

The first word Allah said to the Prophet (Peace Be Upon Him) was Iqra, *Read*. In Islam, acquiring knowledge is mandatory, something some have forgotten because of colonization. Al-Aleem is The All Knowing, and knowledge is something that was gifted to us starting with Adam and Eve (they were still the same person when the Al-Aleem asked Adam to recite all the names and asked The Angels to bow to them).

Knowledge has been part of the equation of human creation from the very beginning. By seeking knowledge, we move towards Al-Aleem and are able to fulfill our purpose. When I say seeking knowledge, I do not mean getting a PhD within neo-liberal institutions. Knowledge has existed far longer than these institutions have and will remain in place beyond them. We gain knowledge through lived experience, through storytelling, through working with the land and celestial bodies, and so much more.

But we are not asked to seek knowledge alone. Knowledge is a part of our work, but our purpose does not change. There are many today who spend their entire lives gaining knowledge but never stewarding land or caring for others. That is not the assignment. The assignment is to steward land and care for one another. If we do not use knowledge for our purpose, then we have failed.

103 Badi'us-Samaawaati wal-Ard: The Originator of the Heavens and the Earth
104 Fatir Alsamawat Wal'ard: Creator of the heavens and the earth

I write about utopia almost every day, even when I am writing of violence and systemic oppression. I am always witnessing utopia. I witness utopia between the violence, strings of possibilities connecting everything and everyone. The possibilities of utopia are limitless. I practice utopia and work to build a vision of a better world. I imagine a world of collective liberation. I imagine a world without borders, where everyone is honored, where we feel safe and at home in our bodies, minds, and spaces. I imagine a world where resources are equitably redistributed. A world where everyone can thrive.

I like my vision of utopia — and I don't want it to be real. What I mean by that is that I know that the greatest thing I can imagine is the smallest of gifts given to us from Badi'us-Samaawaati wal-Ard. In my healthiest days, my brain can barely process the smallest sliver of magic that exists today, magic so effortlessly accessible in a collectively liberated world. I carry a lot of pride in understanding my limitations in imagining, and I smile writing this. I am not The Originator of The Heavens and The Earth. I am not The Architect of The Heavens and The Earth. I am not The Creator of The Heavens and The Earth-like Fatir Alsamawat Wal'ard.

I'm just human. My role isn't to create and to originate the entirety of existence, and I love that my role is different. My role is to steward land and take care of others. My role is to show up everyday and do a little bit better everyday. Beyond that I control nothing, and I don't yearn for any more control than the role I have. The Heavens and The Earth are so much bigger than me and I feel like a child embraced by a loving parent on a cold night. I don't want to think about taking care of everything I don't understand and know. I want to be loved by Badi

Al-Samawati Wal-Ard and Fatir Al-Samawati Wal-Ard — I am loved by Badi Al-Samawati Wal-Ard and Fatir Al-Samawati Wal-Ard.

43 Al-Kareem: The Most Generous

Abd-Alkareem is a name close to my heart. It translates to servant of The Most Generous. Generosity is a big part of my Palestinian culture, and Islamic culture at large. I love my relationship with generosity, but that wasn't always the case. Years ago, I grew to resent cultural generosity, and in a way, I still do.

I grew up in a generous community, and when I say generous, I mean I grew up in a community built on mutual aid, out of necessity for survival. When my family moved to Jordan after a decade and a half in the global north, we were middle class for the first time. We didn't need mutual aid to survive. Generosity moved from community care to familial obligations. Generosity moved from being collectivist to individualistic within a nuclear family and all its branches. Even the mutual aid taking place catered to family. Everyone served the family — not the community.

In *whispers beneath the orange grove*, I have an essay about what collectivism means, and how it differs from individualism. I share that a focus on *our* loved ones is still part of individualism, not collectivism. Collectivism is when we see ourselves as part of an entire community, not just our own personal slice of it.

To be generous is not about what you give. Generosity is a state of being. Generosity is community care. If I buy you a new phone that you do not need — a phone children in the Congo are being killed for — that is not generosity, even if I struggle to afford this phone. Generosity is a practice of being with one another. To be generous is to give and take in harmony as we move towards collective liberation and beyond.

Allah is Al-Kareem The Most Generous, but it's not about the cars or houses or whatever else capitalism tells you constitutes generosity. Al-Kareem gives us everything that we need along the way, allowing us to be part of an ecosystem of care that moves us towards our purpose: stewarding the land and caring for one another.

84 Malik Al-Mulk: The Ruler of All Creation

Ownership comes up repeatedly in the names of Allah, affirming that we do not own anything. Malik is a term used for kings or royalty, but it's rooted in ownership. In a way, royalty is ownership of a people, a land, or both. Al-Mulk are the things that are owned. In this regard, it refers to Allah as The Ruler, or Owner of All Creation, for creation is Allah's to own. There is no shared ownership. Allah is The Only Owner, The Only Ruler, everyone else is playing a role, trying to be something they can never be.

What does it mean to not own anything? Not land, not houses, not children, not family, not relationships, not even our bodies or minds. What does it mean to exclusively only own our decisions? How would we show up differently?

Our egos are tied to all the things we supposedly own: work, art, practice. What does it mean to own a choice but none of the things we enact choices upon? I can choose to do a physical practice that impacts my body. I can choose to get drunk every day. I can choose to get a massage. The list goes on and on, and every decision impacts my body, my mind, and countless other things I do not own.

When I acknowledge that I own my decisions but not the outcomes, and that these decisions have impact, then I recognize decision-making is a responsibility. My decisions are mine to make, but I have a responsibility that extends far beyond my ownership of choice. That responsibility is what differentiates collectivism from individualism. That responsibility is what determines whether or not we accept our role as stewards and caretakers of the planet and one another. We choose to accept this responsibility or not. Every choice either moves us towards The Right Path, or away from The Right Path. Ultimately, what we own is a decision for whether or not we move towards The Right Path, and this decision impacts the entire world.

Chapter 7: Non-Attachment

Art by Yaffa AS

56 Al-Waliyy: The Guardian, The Caretaker

The best and strongest relationship I've ever had is with Allah. I have not lived an easy life, and with every move, it felt like I was being saved from something.

I would have continued to be abused if we didn't leave Jordan.
I would have died if we had stayed in Arizona.
I would have lost everything that I became if we had stayed in Canada.
I would have died if I had stayed in Amman.

The list goes on and on. A lot of it is related to death. These sound dramatic, but I have no doubt that by moving, my life was saved countless times, more times than I can recollect. I haven't had many people supporting me throughout my childhood and early adulthood. But I always had Al-Waliyy.

Al-Waliyy is The Guardian, the one that you relinquish all control to and have such unimaginable faith in them that you know things will always be for the best. Even when it feels like it's too much, I know it's for the best — Al-Waliyy always chooses what's best for us. I don't pretend to know everything. I do not yearn to know everything. What I do know is that The Caretaker is taking care of it.

Al-Waliyy represents non-attachment in all its brilliant facets. Non-attachment is releasing control of the things that we do not control.

Two years ago, as I was claiming non-attached language and expanding the ways it moved in my life, I realized that I had started using non-attachment only when things were difficult. In particular, I was attempting to relinquish control over my relationship with my family — specifically some of my sisters that want to claim whiteness through transphobia. I realized that non-attachment is not just about the sisters I had conflict with. Non-attachment is also about the healthy relationships I have with my parents and others. Non-attachment is not just being okay with losing people I don't really like. It's knowing that I could be on a different path than my parents and any other relationship I yearn for. Non-attachment is knowing that maybe tomorrow I will stop talking to my best friend. Faith in Al-Waliyy is knowing that if I stop talking to my best friend, it is for the best. And maybe, 20 years from now, we'll be best friends again, or we may never speak again. I know nothing. I have all the faith in Al-Waliyy.

Having faith in Al-Waliyy doesn't mean I don't make decisions and make an effort. My role is to show up, what happens beyond that is for Al-Waliyy.

76 Al-Baten: The Hidden

What do you really know about the world? What do I really know?

I have written books and talked on hundreds of stages, lived in ten countries, traveled to over 70, spoken in front of hundreds of thousands, AND I know so little, both in comparison and independently. We know almost nothing as humans, and I embrace so much joy due to this reality.

What is free will if you already know the future, if you know all the past? The joy in free will is in not knowing what comes next. The joy exists in our life journeys through growth, connection, and expansion.

We can be strategic and have comprehensive analysis, but at the end of the day, we never know what will happen. We can plan meticulously, yet we will still end up with results we could have never comprehended. Allah knows all, Allah is all that is visible and invisible. Only The Hidden knows all.

It is in this knowledge that we can move towards non-attachment, relinquishing control. When we believe that we know we are feeding our egos and creating ourselves to be something that we are not, that we must be in control. We have never been in control.

Embrace the hidden and find non-attachment.

90 Al-Maani: The One Who Prevents

The concept of free will fascinates me. Everyone wants it, but only when it makes us feel good. Not when a select few create systems of oppression that genocide hundreds of millions over hundreds of years. I get it — I don't want these systems either, but to want it and seek divine intervention instead of action does not make sense to my autistic brain. It has never made sense. This is different from saying prayer is completely irrelevant. Prayer is intention setting, it is voicing utopia and liberation. Prayer lives in our bodies. Prayer is rewiring our minds to be able to move towards what we pray for. We pray because we know Allah has all the authority, all the power: the only one who can harm, who can heal, and so much more. We know that Allah gave us the responsibility to steward this land and to take care of one another, so we pray and rise in action.

We pray, rise in action, and know that if something does not happen, it was never meant to.
We pray, we rise in action, we move in non-attachment, never knowing outcomes and timelines.
We do it anyway, never knowing if we will actually be liberated.

This begs the question: Who can protect you? Who can prevent harm from ever touching you? Who can prevent systems of oppression from ever forming? Who can move us into a fully liberated world?

None of us can prevent anything. We can strategize and take action, but to prevent something fully is not attainable to us. I can try to plan out 100% of my day to the second and, yet, it will never actually follow my plan. If I am meant to be stuck in traffic, I will be even if I leave at the one time that for years did not have any traffic. I can plan all the events but don't control if any of the planes will depart or arrive on time. I could be across the street from a venue and never make it inside. I can not prevent anything from happening, let alone prevent it from happening in other people's lives.

Patriarchy is built on the idea that cis-males are to provide and protect the rest of us. That's a very kind definition of patriarchy — I know, but the essence is true. Cis-males fail every day, so instead have adopted the more insidious parts of patriarchy in an attempt to achieve it or just because power is alluring. They work to control the rest of us, attempting to control outcomes that they will never be able to control. This is not to say that cis-men largely are operating from this definition and are trying to care for the rest of us nor am I saying most of them have even considered this.

Systems of oppression are dangerous in many ways. They attempt to gaslight us into believing that they are natural and have always been here. The concept of nature is something that is often seen as unquestionable and universal. In fact, questioning systems of oppression is often punished because in understanding we easily recognize the lies. Systems of oppression allure with control. White people have said that they were God — that even God can not sink the Titanic. Control is not real because we can not prevent anything since we never had control of these things in the first place. We make choices, but a choice does not guarantee an outcome. No one but Allah can guarantee an outcome, no matter how small or large.

77 Al-Waali: The Guardian (Mother)

Al-Waali does not actually translate to The Mother. The word is often understood in patriarchal terms these days — often a male is the waali of the family. Historically, clan chiefs were the waali. In some indigenous cultures, such as nation tribes on Turtle Island and Bedouin clans in North Africa, it was elderly women who were the waali. Today, most of our societies give this responsibility to males. Much of patriarchy is built from the abuse of this concept. Patriarchy assumes men as the caretakers (material providers) and protectors, and, thus, are meant to dominate. But the world is hard, and very few can actually provide materially or protect within white supremacist imperialism, and even outside it.

The role of The Guardian is not a role of domination. The role Allah plays can never be compared to a role that humans can, for we are imperfect.

Waali comes from Wala, which means to relinquish. When we say Allah is Al-Wali, we are saying that we have faith in Allah's ability to care for us, for only Allah can.

Ya Allah, inni walaitu laka amri faini la uhsin al ta'awil — Oh Allah I relinquish control for I do not control.

It is our egos that tell us that we have control. It is systems of oppression that tell us we must have control. To have faith in Allah as Al-Waali is to relinquish control that was never ours — it is to move into non-attachment. Systems of oppression lie to us and tell us we are in control of ourselves and of others. When we believe that we have control, and we are guardians, we restrict the endless possibilities of humanity. The logic is one we see often for the sake of "safety," "protection," and whatever else is "best for you," assuming that someone truly knows what's best for us. Only Al-Waali truly knows what's best.

89 Al-Mughni: The Enricher

Systems of oppression are rooted in control. Liberation is the practice of submission and non-attachment, not control. Within systems of oppression, we are taught we control the things that enrich us, specifically in a material context. For example, we are taught that if we work hard enough, we will be wealthy and be afforded healthcare, housing, food, and luxurious vacations. We are taught that if we are enriched materially, then everything else will fall into place.

Systems of oppression have created structures of control that to an extent allow accessing material differently depending on who you are. How you assimilate into whiteness and other systems of oppression will impact how you are able to accumulate wealth and other resources. I witnessed this in my childhood in Oidbaḍ Do'ag (colonized name Tempe AZ), as Arab and South Asian families were able to move out of poverty with relative ease compared to Black and Indigenous folks. But at the end of the day, only Al-Mughni is The Enricher.

I made the most amount of money between the ages of 23 and 25. I had three full time jobs (Quality Engineer at a Fortune 500, Director of Mental Health at a non-profit, and Peer Support Certification Trainer across various states), making nearly $120,000 a year between 2015 and 2018. I ended up in $30,000 in medical debt due to my deteriorating physical and mental health, lived in my car for 18 months due to community violence, and barely survived. From 2019 to 2020, I made about $40,000. I got out of debt, had housing, and finally began to breathe. Systems of oppression will never actually take care of us, only Allah can and does.

This is not to say Allah rewards and punishes on a daily basis as is commonly known sometimes. It is to say Allah granted us the responsibility of stewarding this earth and taking care of one another, and within that, built unlimited pathways for enrichment. Everything is already here. It is in our abuse of these systems as a species that we no longer have what we need. The planet has everything for us: enough food, enough water, enough oxygen, enough everything. Some humans have created systems for inequitable distribution attempting to become the enrichers, but they will never be — all they lead to is destruction, misery, and injustice.

9 Al-Azeez: The Almighty

Al-Azeez is the name that is used most frequently in the Quran, with 92 counts. In many translations, The All Mighty is described as The Powerful/The Conqueror, but Allah does not need to conquer anything. Al-Azeez is not The All Mighty because in less than an instant, all creation can be erased, or an entire universe of new creation can be formed. It's that we are incapable of ever reaching a level where we can threaten Al-Azeez. Al-Azeez is beyond any harm that we can cause.

When someone has Ezat nafs (عزة نفس), roughly translating to "pride/honor in one's self," we are saying that they are untouchable — you can't harm them even if you tried. This can have a negative connotation if the pride/honor is built through ego. If pride/honor is built on genuine spiritual connection and non-attachment, then we cannot be harmed through our ego (this not saying all harm is ego related but a lot of harm is rooted in ego).

I think about this in terms of state violence. The state can assassinate, incarcerate, disappear, and do many other things to us. So what if the state can kill and disappear us?

I even think about it in terms of individuals in my life. I learned long ago that my family, teachers, friends, co-workers, and co-organizers will not validate my life. I learned whether I did the things they told me to or the opposite, I could not control their approval. Their dismissal and approval are irrelevant to me. I am not saying that folks can't hold me accountable — that's different. I am saying that societal approval is irrelevant to me because it's not real. The only approval I care about is Al-Azeez's.

16 Al-Qahhar: The One That Has Control of All

We use the word Qahher to describe a feeling beyond pain, beyond anger in Palestinian culture. It is an emotion in response to inhumane harm. Qahher is similar to rage but is something far more dangerous. Rage is an emotion that helps us transform. It's an emotion that demands action and realignment of our values. Rage exists anytime an injustice occurs and demands that we do something about that injustice. Similar to any emotion if we do not process it in a healthy way, it can be destructive in non-strategic ways. Qahher on the other hand is that bridge between resentment and rage. Because its cause is inhumane, there is no level of action that will satisfy it.

I write this the morning of New Years Day 2025. Over the last 24 hours, I thought I had been reflecting on non-attached rage, and I realize now that what I have actually been reflecting on is non-attached qahher. Within Palestinian families we say, "they died from qahher." We know qahher is a thing that moves in our bodies in destructive ways and does in fact kill many of us. We call it "the silent killer." My people have experienced such inhumane pain on a huge scale that dying from that pain seems almost like a gift.

I have been reflecting on qahher because I feel it moving through my veins, exacerbating stomach problems gifting me ulcers, firming my neck-shoulder-back muscles, and, just this morning at Fajr, I sneezed, and it felt as if I dislocated the right side of my back. I write this in severe bodily pain.

Yesterday, during a workshop with the fabulous Alice Sparkly Kat, they asked us to sketch in a minute what each of the seasons of 2024 were like for us. The first thing that came up for me for all the seasons is anger, so much anger that I recognize as qahher now. All the magical things of 2024 were overshadowed by the severe injustices that found no home through accountability. During the last year I have witnessed state violence impacting my communities directly and witnessed community violence tear us apart. I have been carrying so much qahher, just like the rest of my people. Because I haven't done the work to move towards a non-attached practice for qahher, it has lived in my body my entire life.

Since that session, I have been thinking about what non-attached qahher would look like. In most areas of my life, I have a non-attached practice. I know I can't control what will happen and what will not. To the point that I don't claim to know where I'll live moving forward, or what work I'll do, or which books I'll write, or anything at all. I do things, but I'm not attached to any of them. This book is meant to be released Feb 14th, 2025, but for all I know it may never be released, and I am absolutely okay with that. In fact, I love that. What's meant to be will be.

When it comes to qahher, though, I have been trying to define where my rage, anger, and resentments go and build out exact equations for releasing it through the work I do. I have defined it to the point of attachment. When we attach it means we close off the pathways that would actually allow us to release, keeping everything tangled inwardly and where eventually it will fall apart or destroy us. It's destroyed me before and it may yet again — I don't control that. What I do control as an awareness and desire to want to expand my non-attached practice to qahher. I don't know what that looks like, but I am no longer resisting it.

This morning, instead of writing at home or at a coffee shop, I was called to write in the middle of a redwood grove. Everything feels lighter here. In the face of something so inhumane, we must turn to our purpose for being here. We cannot steward the land without a relationship with the land. Land understands qahher, and it knows how to move through it, connected to every millimeter of soil. Connecting with land grounds things like qahher because we are no longer carrying this alone. Qahher would not exist if we had larger scale community support. The wound of qahher exists because injustice happens, and then we are in a void where it seems like no one can hear us. We are alone in qahher and cannot possibly comprehend that anyone else can relate. We fear relating to qahher because if others can relate, then things are as bad in reality as they are in our imagination. What if we still don't feel better when we come together? So, we separate and move deeper into the abyss without the foundation to be able to claim the abyss and all that lies within it.

Allah is Al-Qahhar. I think in a lot of ways I used to think about this attribute as one of the attributes we are meant to stay away from at all costs. People who move away from Al-Qahhar cause injustice and inflict severe harm. You can NOT enact genocide from a love ethic — don't argue with me. We are not meant to be okay when injustice happens to us and around us. Qahher is a deep level of awareness that shows us the work we can do and reminds us at the same time that Only Al-Qahhar is The One That Has Control of All. We have so little control, but moving towards Al-Qahhar is always going to provide us with what we need. Qahher like any other emotion is not evil. Everything comes from Allah.

58 Al-Muhsee: The Assessor

I come across tens of thousands of people a year during my events. Some years, it can be in the hundreds of thousands. Most days, I can barely remember the names of the handful of loved ones in my life. Birthdays and details about people's lives are no longer easy to remember. Every year I remember less. Yet, people still share things with me — incredibly beautiful and profound things. And they know I will most likely not remember any of it. Even then, if they share the most important parts of their lives, I know almost nothing about them. I am a single ship in an ocean of 8 billion ships, and I cross paths with more of them in a year than most people will in their entire lives. And yet, I know nothing about them — and those are the ones still alive. My brain cannot comprehend processing the lives of every human that has ever existed. My limitations are a constant reminder of the power of Al-Muhsee.

Al-Muhsee assesses and knows every single detail of every single life, even beyond humans. There isn't a single thing that's forgotten along the way. Allah knows everything that has ever existed and has not existed.

Recognizing Al-Muhsee's ability to witness everyone allows my anxiety to settle and allows me to move towards relinquishing what I do not control through non-attachment. I don't need to remember everyone or show up for everyone, because no one is ever truly alone, no one is invisible and irrelevant to Al-Muhsee.

14 Al-Musawer: The Fashioner of Forms

In Arabic, Musawer means photographer.

Non-attachment is realizing we don't have control of the vast majority of things, and most importantly, we don't know how things will turn out — we can't predict the final form of anything, not even ourselves. I can look in the mirror and witness both my parents staring back at me, but that doesn't necessarily mean I'll look anything like them when I'm in my early 60's. Only Al-Musawer knows. I can try to force a certain thing, but there's no telling if it will happen, and what it will end up looking like.

This shows up in every aspect of our lives. I didn't know where I would be writing today. I didn't know if I would be writing. My initial plan was to have this written three days ago, but that wasn't what happened. Technically the plan was to actually finish this book a month ago, but a third of the way through, a YA fantasy novel wanted to be written instead. Who am I to say no?

I recognize that within capitalism, not everyone can operate from that same standpoint. If you have a submission deadline, you may not have the capacity to shift and write another book before returning to the original. This is another reminder about how capitalism is constantly attempting to move us away from Al-Musawer and our nature. Non-attachment is human. Capitalism tells us to control is to be human, which is something that can never be true.

There's no guarantee that you will practice non-attachment in a world where systemic oppression exists, but what we do control is our own decisions, and how we attempt to move in the world. By embracing non-attachment as a practice and moving towards Al-Musawer, we move beyond these systems where yes they will threaten us and punish us but it doesn't matter anymore because they don't have any actual power. I don't embrace non-attachment because I am wealthy (sounds gross even writing it) — I embrace non-attachment because I know what the worst thing these systems can do to us, and I will take that any day as long as I am connected to Al-Musawer.

I have experienced houselessness, severe food insecurity, all kinds of health problems, and loss of family and friends. I would do that all again to counter a single moment when I am not connected to Al-Musawer. When I am connected to Al-Musawer, I live in a world of endless possibilities. When I move away, it is the only time I feel alone, unworthy, and disposable. Systems of oppression try to make me feel those things all the time, but it is only moving away from Al-Musawer that actually makes me feel that.

I choose to practice non-attachment, knowing that I don't define that and don't know what that looks like — and that's non-attachment.

72 Al-Muakher: The Delayer & 71 Al-Muqadem: The Advancer

Ever since I was a teenager, my favorite prayer has been, "Oh Allah, please do whatever is best for me." At some point, I stopped asking for specific things, and prayed for the best instead. I changed this prayer twice. Two times in my life I changed it to, "Oh Allah, please let this be the best thing for me." The first time was while I was trying to leave Jordan for college. The second was when I was getting my first job after graduation at a fortune 500. I have thought of changing the prayer since then, but nothing in particular feels worthy to ask for it to exist in the way I want it to.

If I had gotten everything I've ever wanted at the time I wanted it, my life would've looked very different. I don't believe it would be different in a good way — although everything is meant to be, and it would have been meant to be. I love where I am in life. I love that I have not received all I wanted because I learned it was not the best for me instead. I am grateful that certain things I wanted were delayed, and others were advanced. I am grateful that I do not control outcomes.

If you had gotten all that you ever wanted when you wanted it, what would your life look like?

If I had gotten what I wanted with this book then you would have read different words nine years ago. Nine years ago is multiple worlds ago, and I have faith that you will read these words when you are meant to, and the words that are meant to reach you will when they are meant to. They may be delayed, and they may be advanced. It is beyond me.

99 As-Sabur: The Patient One

Although there is no exact order to the 99 names of Allah, they are often listed in order of importance that someone after the prophet's death determined. As-Sabur (The Patient One) is often listed last on most lists, while Ar-Rahman (The Most Merciful) is listed first.

My name was changed the moment I was born, and Mama gifted me a different name. It's not entirely clear why my mom changed a name that had been given to me nearly a decade before I was born — she saw me, and it was done. The exchanged name was "Ayoub," after Prophet Ayoub, or Prophet Job in Christianity. Prophet Ayoub was known for patience. I used to joke that Mama looked at me, exhausted months after being displaced with two other million Palestinians to Jordan from Kuwait post the Gulf War, said f*%k patience, and gifted me a name for praise and transformation.

I used to view patience as passivity. If you were patient, you were idle, never taking action, never striving. You were waiting. Over the years, this developed a resentment towards the concept of patience. Patience became the vision of people refusing to take the most basic of actions.

A few years ago, I picked up the Sufi tarot deck (ended up with three decks because two friends know me well, and I had already gotten one), and during my winter solstice draw for myself, I pulled the Sabr card. The Sabr card in the Sufi tarot represents the Temperance card in the Major Arcana Tarot. Temperance is a card of balance "as above so below." It struck me then that patience is balance, it is a deep-rootedness in the elements and transcendence, in perfect harmony. This card draw was during a time when it felt like I was losing all that I am as a caretaker to a chosen family member who was dying from stage four cancer. Patience all of a sudden became about having balance as I moved through life.

Over time, as I continued to claim non-attachment, I have learned that the balance in patience is in fact non-attachment. Patience is not meant to be passive. Patience is recognizing the power we have, and that we do not control time. We do not control when things will or if they will happen at all. I can make all the plans I want, but at the end of the day, there are infinite amounts of things that I do not control. Things will be. That is non-attachment, achieved only when we are balanced.

Patience does not say to never act and passively wait for life to happen. We may take action, we may strive, we may dream, we may move, but we can never control the outcome.

Allah, however, does control the outcome, implying that the balance transcends non-attachment. Allah controls outcomes and, yet, we are granted free choice. We make choices everyday that move us towards or away from Allah. Allah remains perfectly balanced, connected to us and everything else endlessly. There is no wavering. Allah is balance, Allah is patience.

Sabr in Arabic is also the name of cacti (just a silly fun fact).

Chapter 8: Power - Claiming Humanity

Art by Yaffa AS

70 Al-Muqtader: The All Powerful

Within systems of oppression, power is seen as something you exert over things. In the same way, many understand Al-Muqtader through the power of oppression and punishment.

In many of my workshops and events, I ask attendees if they truly know what power they have. Some of my favorite intensive training sessions are about understanding and claiming power.

When I am asked during events what people can do to organize, my answer is always to understand and claim your power. I don't say understand and claim your privilege — although that can be a part of liberation work. The power I am referencing is our inherent power. Before systems of oppression, were we not powerful? Our power has existed as long as we have, perhaps even before in the early stages of creation as Angels wondered why we would exist at all.

The thing is: Allah exists beyond the systemic oppression that we created. Allah does not need to oppress and to punish us to be powerful. If true power is love and compassion and mercy then The All Powerful is The Most Loving, The Compassionate, The Most Merciful — all names of Allah.

Our inherent power comes from our love, compassion, care, warmth — everything good in us. Power through systemic oppression is power built from the oppression of others, but it is power that we have as long as we live in systemically oppressive societies. We may use the power given to us from oppressive systems to help dismantle them, but a collectively liberated world is only built through our inherent power.

And sure, Al-Muqtader can oppress and punish if Allah wishes, but that's not what makes Allah powerful. Even in a world where Allah is branded as a punisher, far more people believe in Divinity from a place of love, not a place of fear of punishment.

78 Al-Muta'ali: The Most Exalted

Allah is Al-Muta'ali, the only one above everything that has and will ever exist. There is no equal or competition. We are not even in the competition if there ever was one, for all the contenders would be the 99 names of Allah.

Years ago, while conducting peer support certification training, I remember beginning to redefine humility as "knowing the awesomeness within me and being able to honor awesomeness within you." This was after years of being told to bring myself down, so white-cis-straight people would feel comfortable around my magic. As someone who was supposedly perceived as a Muslim male (only when whiteness was uncomfortable with my gender), I had to practice making myself small to cater to whiteness. I changed how loud I would be, to the point that I can't bring myself to be loud outside of a laughing yoga session today. I added "um's" and "like's" into my sentences to phrase statements as questions, allowing them (the privileged in the room) to perceive that they were the decision makers. Not only is it my autism that makes me good at navigating systems of oppression, it's also that I have always had to survive them.

Within the mental health world, I realized that we punished wellness more than despair for the global-majority queer and trans disabled people. When we make ourselves small, they make themselves feel better by hypothetically elevating us. They are the saviors after all. This obviously did not work for my Leo nature. Save me? I laugh at Helsinki airport, even now as I write this, eating a forkful of cake and sipping coffee.

Marginalized folks are most dangerous when we recognize and understand our power. When we do, we are to be treated as a threat — rightfully so — to a system that knows it cannot survive beneath our light. Saviorism is white supremacy in action; it gaslights us into believing that the ones who harm are, in fact, the ones helping. It also reinforces that power only exists through oppression, and marginalized people don't have it without assimilating into oppressive systems.

It fascinates me that people can think they are above others on such a scale. How sad it is to think you are above someone when the only thing making you less is that belief, not because we see you as less, but because you've robbed yourself of the magic that exists beyond you.

60 Al-Mueed: The Restorer

Humans are arrogant — that is not up for debate. We believe that we matter so much that we commit genocide, femicide, and wreak havoc to the planet. On the other hand, many believe that humans are capable of ending humanity or fully destroying the world. We are so inconsequential.

Over the last 15 months, so many around me have asked what would happen if they killed every single person in Gaza, believing that zionists can achieve such a thing, as if there won't always be people from Gaza, regardless of what zionists and other fascists believe. We witness the planet fighting back. Everything can be restored if Al-Mueed wills it to. We may believe something is eternal, but nothing but Allah is.

I write this a couple of weeks after Bashar Al-Assad left Syria, something that so many thought was impossible in our lifetimes. Yet, it happened. One day, we woke up, and it had happened — of course, countless people have been working for years to make it happen. I and so many others do not know if the loved ones that disappeared over the last 14 years are still alive or not, but it did happen.

The world will end. And yes, humans in the last 500 years have been bad stewards of land. But the world ending will not be about us, for we might kill, but we cannot end anything. We do not have that kind of power.

What does it mean to have restoration after genocide? What does it mean for Syrians to wake up without a dictator governing their every move? What does it mean for any place that systemic oppression has destroyed to be restored?

We see the ocean claiming ships that have harmed it. We see trees growing where they were not welcome for generations, reclaiming structures left behind to time. We see fires reclaiming hills and mountains. We see floods claiming back what was always theirs.

I think about the chemicals in Gaza right now. I wonder how zionists would do that to the land, steal it, and then want to live there. Then, I remember that Allah is Al-Mueed, and if Gaza is meant to be restored, it will be — no human can stop it. I recognize my limitations, and how little power I have in the face of all this. I know that my role is to act and show up, but all of it is beyond me.

59 Al-Mubdi': The Originator

Mubdi' stems from to begin or initiate. There is nothing in creation that exists without Al-Mubdi. This is a concept that is easily manipulated to blame Al-Mubdi for things like genocide. Yes, nothing exists without Allah, but we are beings with free will. Genocide is a choice, a human choice. Al-Mubdi' has no need for genocide. If Allah wants a people gone, they can be erased from existence instantaneously. The decisions we make are ours to make, but everything originates from Al-Mubdi'. Nothing exists without Allah — nothing.

10 Al-Jabbar: The Compeller/The Restorer

I feel immense sorrow in how certain concepts have been weaponized within systemic oppression.

As I sit here, I think about all the times in my life when I knew what was best for me, and I really didn't want to do it. I was tired sometimes; I was in pain at other times; and I still wanted to be in pain a bit longer before moving most of the time.

As much as I know about my life, as much as free will is beautiful, I am actually not the best person to govern every aspect of my life. If I actually made every single decision in my life, my life would be a nightmare to be honest. If my younger self got what they wanted, they would have assimilated into whiteness, into cis-ness, into straightness, into being able-bodied, into…the gross list goes on and on. If it wasn't for the circumstances of my life, I may not have written these words. I am grateful for every part of my life I have not controlled, and all the choices I have made.

I love the balance between what I make decisions about, and the things that are beyond me.

I did not have a say in what I was born into: family, land, body, and so many other things. I was born an autistic, queer, trans, Palestinian Muslim into a family displaced multiple times through various wars — I was born perfect (I'm not being sarcastic, I'm drinking a ginger fennel chai right now, and I know who I am). I was born into a world that would try to do everything it can to diminish that perfection. I couldn't control any of these things. Even as a child, moving across continents, I had no say in the first 13 years of my life. Even as an adult, navigating immigration systems, police brutality, systemic violence, and so many more decisions were made for me by these systems.

Systems of oppression desire to be Al-Jabbar, to be the ones who compel everything, but in reality, they try and they fail. I know they fail because I am still an autistic, queer, trans, Palestinian Muslim, and I am perfect! Read that again, and tell me that these systems have not failed.

Al-Jabbar is The Compeller and compels everything in existence in ways that we will never understand in beautiful and profound ways, and sometimes it looks horrible from the outside. But it is magical, and I am beyond grateful for it. Al-Jabbar can also translate to The Restorer. This is where systems of oppression fail. Compelling without restoring is an imbalance. Al-Jabbar compels everything into restoration, maintaining balance that we can not comprehend.

When I submit to Al-Jabbar, recognizing the power I have and all the things I do not control, I allow my life to be restored. Some days it may seem as if everything has fallen apart in the world, but I believe that things fall apart to be restored. In an essay I wrote three weeks after Oct 7th 2023, published in *Whispers Beneath the Orange Grove* (2024, Meraj Publishing), I wrote:

"In the last three weeks, every one of my identities has been weaponized as a way to justify my people's

genocide, my genocide. You might wonder, how can I think of Utopia as the world is falling apart? It is as the world falls that it is made anew. As a death doula, I know that death is a beginning. Mourn the old world and usher in a new one. Let it be a better world."

I still stand by these words a year and a half later.

26 Al-Mudhil: The Giver of Disgrace

There is no glory nor grace without Allah. There are many who deserve disgrace and to fall from any kind of grace. Ultimately, it is Al-Mudhil who is The Giver of Disgrace. Al-Mudhil is not waiting for you to mess up to disgrace you. Al-Mudhil does not wait. As someone moves away from Al-Mudhil, they are automatically moving towards the cliff of disgrace.

When I think of disgrace, I think of shame. I think about how within a white gaze, shame is seen as this horrible thing that incapacitates us. In reality, shame is transformative. Shame is a feeling we experience when we are not values aligned or when our values are harmful to our purpose (stewarding the land and caring for one another) in the world.

Shame is what happens when we are moving away from Al-Mudhil. When we start acting from a place of lovelessness, lack of compassion and grace and kindness, we experience shame. In many ways, shame is an emotion that asks us to move back towards Al-Mudhil when we have lost track of The Right Path. Shame is not our enemy. In fact, shame is an emotion we should yearn for on our journeys as it highlights the areas where we are not living up to where we are meant to be.

50 Al-Baa'ith: The Restorer of Life

I grew up believing that the name Baa'ith, the time we all are raised from the dead, is about accountability. After living our lives, while being witnessed throughout, nothing lost or forgotten, we return for accountability. Many believe that individuals are thrown into Hell or Heaven, but for me, it's about Al-Haqq (The Truth).

I want to know the truth. I want to understand what I am not able to fully understand in this body-mind. And even though a part of me wants vengeance against those committing genocide and mass atrocities, I want to know about the everyday people who have harmed me most. We may feel we are moving in a certain direction and then find ourselves shocked into another.

I want to understand beyond my current capabilities. I want to fully understand how I have shown up and the harm that I have caused, and I want to learn from it. I believe growth continues beyond this single life and has been happening for countless generations before.

Only Al-Baa'ith can help us fulfill this cycle. Only Al-Baa'ith restores life, life that Al-Baa'ith is the only One capable of giving in the first place.

5 Al-Qudoos: The Most Holy

Is there anything that systemic oppression has not desecrated? Can systems of oppression survive in a world where the sacred is untouched?

What does it mean to be holy, to be sacred?

Several months ago at an event in Norway for my book *desecrated poppies,* an attendee asked what desecrated meant. I went into the depth of what it meant to me, and then another incredible participant added that it was simply to violate the sacred.

Today, I wonder what in fact is sacred.

I am a death and birthing worker. I witness many parts of our lives that we view as sacred, such as birth and death and marriage. I am also in community with sex workers, and a part of the pro-sex movement. In many ways, within religious contexts, sex is seen as holy. Purity intersects with ownership through the concept of virginities. Sex, even more so than birth and death, is holy, so sacred that it must be hidden away and disappeared. Sex is about life and death. Life happens through death. Sex is the death of purity. And in more extreme traditions, sex warrants death. The AIDS epidemic showed us profoundly what punishment for sex looked like in a White, Christian, Nationalist, Global North.

The thing with the oppression of the mind is that it targets everyday people, like you and I. Or even my mom. I think of conversations with her early on about queerness and transness. Even when I brought up how we were killed, she always ended with, "but you're not like them." To her, non-hetero sex outside of a marriage is worse than murdering us. Unfortunately, there are far more extreme people out there than my mom, and she has come around to understand how awful of a statement that was.

If Al-Qudoos is Everything Holy, then everything in creation is by extension holy, specifically the parts of us that remember our connection to Al-Qudoos. Life is holy. The breath flowing through and out of my lungs is holy because it moves me closer to Al-Qudoos.

It is not sex that is holy. It is not death or birth. Everything that moves us towards Al-Qudoos is holy. It is not sex that desecrates us. We are holy because Al-Qudoos willed it.

Everything can be liberatory. Sex can be liberatory, or it can extend oppressions. Death and birth can be liberatory or weaponized. Everything can move us towards or away from Al-Qudoos.

Al-Qudoos is The Only The Most Holy, in a constant state of being holy and sacred. The rest of us flow between stages as we navigate our lives and move towards The Right Path.

42 Al-Jaleel: The Most High/Honourable

Hierarchies, in all areas of life, fascinate me. Hierarchies come up in my work whether through one on one work, family and group work, or with organization and communities. Hierarchies also come up within interpersonal relationships.

Many of the organizations and communities I have supported over the last 15 years have desired consensus-based models and horizontal leadership structures as opposed to hierarchical structures. Hierarchical structures are generally when you have a specific chain of command. Horizontal structures on the other hand have limited layers of management and are often referred to as a flat structure. Consensus-based models usually refer to decision making where decisions are made collectively and agreement is required in a consensus for decisions to be made. A consensus-based model can work across both models of leadership structures.

Systems of oppression have taught us that a hierarchy is bad and will always be abusive, whereas consensus-based structures are remedies to systems of oppression. The messaging saying that consensus and horizontal structures are equitable and move us towards collective liberation comes from these same systems.

This is not a pro-authoritarianism reflection. This is a reflection that any and all structures are abusive and will be weaponized against the most marginalized within systems of oppression. For example, an organization I supported had a consensus-based, horizontal decision-making structure before I supported them. For any decision, all members of the organization came together to make decisions. They thought they were equitable However, when you look at who is in the room, you realize that the least paid person is the one trans-Black person, getting paid $60K less than the executive director making the same decisions (non-trans and not Black). This was an abusive structure.

I prefer hierarchical structures. Hierarchical structures do not have to be evil. If everyone is paid the same, and you utilize structures in place where no one can abuse their power, it actually allows everyone to be honored for what they're bringing to the table. This does not create a hierarchy about role importance, and it allows individuals to lean into their skill sets and expertise instead of assuming everyone is going to bring the same thing to the table. Hierarchical structures, when done properly, can allow the individuals most impacted to have the largest say in decisions impacting them. Horizontal structures and consensus-based decision-making can be equitable, but the process is very different. The biggest threat to equitable structures is assuming equity is automatically built into them.

Any structure can be weaponized within systems of oppression, and any structure can be used to counter systems of oppression. There are ways to make consensus-based and horizontal models equitable. However, I find that many individuals working towards movement building are more inclined to have a basic, binary understanding of good and evil.

A hierarchy is bad when people with power have authority over marginalized lives and assert their power over us. By understanding our power and removing the benefits to aligning with capitalism we build truly equitable structures where no human is above another. Because no human is above another.

Only Al-Jaleel is above everything in creation. We might have different roles, but all creation is equal. Angels might seem so much greater than humans, but they are not above us. Angels have a role to play and Humans have a role to play. The land has a role to play. Only Al-Jaleel is above us all.

53 Al-Wakeel: The One in Charge (Caretaker)

اللهم إني وكلتك أمري فأنت لي خير وكيل.

Oh Allah, I have submitted my being to you for you are the best caretaker

Al-Wali is the one who is given tawkeel, which is the responsibility of care. Al-Wakeel extends what Al-Wali does and grants responsibility of care. As humans, when guardianship and responsibility of care are granted, it is abused sometimes (re: Britney Spears, or most trans and disabled people within a system of care).

Abuse is about control. When one individual or community creates barriers for another individual or community to be all that they can be, then that is abuse. Abuse often implies that one party has more power than the other. However, power within systems of oppression is often an illusion. Abuse is using this illusion to try to make others believe that they are less powerful than they are. If we look at any system of oppression and break down who is privileged and who is marginalized it is rarely an accurate reflection of where power truly lies. For example, the global majority out number white anglo European descendants. The land the global majority are indigenous to carry the vast majority of resources in the world. This applies to every system of oppression.

A few years ago, a friend in Ireland asked if I thought that there genuinely were no gender roles, and he felt that there had to be. He comes from a farming background and I asked what gender roles looked like for his parents. Both parents worked the farm while the mother also did the household and child caretaking. Often, marginalized people have to do the labor of both the privileged and the marginalized.

The power we know that allows us to abuse one another is not a form of power that is real — it's an illusion. The All Powerful doesn't need an illusion to keep us away from our power. There is no competition.

Caretaking is our primary purpose on this planet: to steward the land and care for one another. Abuse will always occur within systems of oppression because they are built on controlling what is not humanities to control.

Al-Wakeel is the only true source of care that is guaranteed, so there can never be an abuse of power.

Some believe in a vengeful God. That says a lot more about the society and communities they stem from than anything else. Al-Wakeel has no need to abuse us and seek vengeance against us for there is no harm we can ever cause Allah. For queer and trans people, we are often told by our own communities that, "when you have gay sex, Allah's throne is shaken." The statement is incredibly ridiculous, and I won't address it beyond this poem from my collection *desecrated poppies:*

***

they say,
God said
we are the worst
in creation.

have they not witnessed genocide?
have they not glimpsed whiteness?
have they not met capitalism?
have they not seen themselves?

***

Allah is our caretaker and is The Only One in Charge — The Only One who can never abuse us.

46 Al-Waasi: The All Encompassing

I have lived my entire life at the borders of possibilities like I have lived on the borders of displacement and navigating dozens of borders worldwide. You see, I don't make sense. I should not be who I am, according to everything commonly believed in society.

I was diagnosed with autism at the age of 5, although moving across an ocean allowed people to forget. To this day, I don't know if the autism diagnosis came due to how my deep childhood trauma was coming forward, or if it was always there — I know it's the latter, but societal voices that have yet to be exorcised make me doubt it sometimes. But I know it does not matter. I was very disassociated as a child, the first time happening at 22 months old and two years prior to the larger childhood abuse. It was rare for me to be present as a child — it felt like I was hated by everyone except Mama, who was terrified of showing any love to the AMAB child of the family. In many ways, I think my mom and I are still on good terms because we recognize the contradictions that exist within us, both yearning and being punished for our yearnings.

I was hated as a child. I cannot stress that point enough, and I despise a world that hates children. I wasn't hated because I was disruptive like other children. The fact we hate children who do not fit into our authoritarian schools and families is disgusting. I was hated because I was different, and different is not very likable. I was not a charismatic child; I had yet to learn to mask to become a charismatic adult. I was a child who listened to directions and faded in the background because the direction was often to shut up.

In the liminal space between invisibility and hypervisibility as an AMAB person, I learned that none of it is real. These barriers and borders that they tell us we must abide by are not real. I have failed every expectation — both the expectations that I would never "succeed" or that I would "succeed" in areas that are seen as basic and easily doable such as talking, reading, writing, or understanding concepts. I have never been basic — I write this while I sip Yemeni chai. I became all that I am not because the world thought I would — I made the world irrelevant. I am who I am with the grace of Al-Waasi'. Al-Waasi' is The All Encompassing. That definition is not quite right. In my head, it's closer to The Vast. Waasi' means vast, but Al-Waasi' is The Abundant, The One Who has No Limits, The One Who Allows us to Expand and move beyond what's seen as possible or impossible.

My life is a living contradiction, only because systems of oppression can't make sense of me. These systems should never be the ones to make sense of us. If we make sense to oppressive systems, then are we truly on The Right Path?

Chapter 9: Right Path

Art by Yaffa AS

98 Ar-Rashid: The Right Path

Rashid comes from the root word Rushd (رُشد), meaning sound judgment or the right path. Rashid is the one who is rightly guided. Ar-Rashid is the One Who Guides to the Right Path.

Rashid was one of my favorite people's last name growing up in Oidbaḍ Do'ag (colonized name Tempe AZ). She was and continues to be one of my sisters — although our paths rarely intersect these years. In a lot of ways, her and one of my older sisters were similar. As children, they were filled with spirit; they filled every room with life and compassion. In adulthood, the world broke them both, and although they still fill every room with life, they are often subdued as if drowning underwater — just out of reach.

Unfortunately, those with the most life, with kindness and love and compassion, are the ones a white supremacist capitalist world targets and does everything to try and destroy.

Ar-Rashid moves us to life, defined as this world, what lies before and lies after. Life is liberatory. Life is meant to be filled with love and compassion, inspiration and passion, liberation and utopia.

Most things in our lives move us away from life, away from Ar-Rashid. The decolonized practice of teaching is meant to move us towards life. Yet, it is often in schools where we often learn to move away from life and instead move towards authoritarian acceptance of capitalism. I choose my words very carefully here because it is not that they block our path to life, for I don't think anyone can really do that — although they may try. But a path moves in different directions. Little by little, we are moved away from the path of life and into the paths of white supremacy, capitalism, patriarchy, ableism, trans-hatred, and so many others. It's not just in our conditioning to these systems that we move away from the path to life. Rather, it's the subtle ways we are broken to allow these systems to always supersede any other paths.

During my sophomore year of college, while working multiple jobs and being overly involved on campus to survive, my past crept up on me, and I ended up with PTSD. It was during a time when I was so overworked and lived with such severe insomnia that I was in a cycle of being over-caffeinated and passing out every few days. I have lost count how many times I have nearly died to survive capitalism. At my breaking point I decided that enough was enough, and that surviving capitalism was not worth anything. I decided that I mattered more. I decided that no matter what I would get eight hours of sleep and a day off a week. Nothing was going to stop me from achieving this and nothing does. I quit coffee, started sleeping, and took my day off. I connected with the land and external community in a way that I had never been able to before. I didn't end up doing less, in fact I excelled.

The Right path is subjective depending on who you talk to. A white-supremacist will tell you white-supremacy is the Right path. A transphobe will tell you the same.

Spirituality is about a universal Right path, beyond anything any man can ever create. Yet, it is spirituality that then gets weaponized and turned against individuals whether through religion, through secularism, or anything in between. The concept that it is only religion that guides us to the Right Path has led to genocide and ethnic cleansing. It is inherently the same concept that allows religion to be used as a tool for the expansion of the colonial project, settler colonialism, genocide, slavery, ethnic cleansing, femicide, and so many other immense forms of violence that are at odds with the Right path.

The Right path is not defined by us. It just is. The Right Path is also not a linear path. If universal consciousness or enlightenment is the top of a mountain, The Right Path then is all the trails that lead to the summit. Some are longer, some are shorter. Some have steeper inclines, others require scrambling and rock climbing. There are countless paths to the one summit. The Right path is all of them. And although the path is one, we can also find ourselves moving away from the summit.

In many ways, Ar-Rashid is telling us that moving towards Oneness is the Right Path, moving towards Allah is the Right path. The names of Allah are what fill these trails, and how we move towards the summit.

Not only do we need to have sabr (patience) with ourselves and others on this path, but we also know that Allah is patient with us as we move towards Allah. I have seen loved ones broken by these systems moving towards life after embracing who they are. These systems try to destroy us but there are far more paths in The Right Path than the paths leading us to soullessness.

34 Al-Atheem: The Great

As I write this, I think about all the white leaders of the last several hundred years who called themselves The Great. I think about how all they have done is create oppressive systems, where they are even miserable themselves. These White Greats created their version of utopia (the world we currently live in), attempting to be creators themselves. How sad. This is the best they could do. And yes, we may suffer immensely because of them, but it shows again and again that they were never The Great. They were never anything more than violent people who were on the wrong path, a path of misery and suffering that they needed to extend to the rest of us. They saw what we had, and they yearned for it, assuming that spiritual cannibalism is the way to get what we have. They fail everyday.

Al-Atheem does not fail. Al-Atheem has created countless worlds across time and space, where we move towards collective liberation despite the harm that these people can do. Only Allah is Al-Atheem, The Great. Everyone else is a basic oppressor that yearns for something they will never get through oppression.

94 Al-Hadi: The One Who Guides

Allah is the Right Path and is the One Who Guides us to and within the Right Path (Ar-Rashid). Allah is the mountain, the trails, the summit, and everything else. It is through Allah that we are all that we are.

Allah guides us in everything. Our intuition, others' voices, and even our ancestors will never 100% accurately guide us, but Allah will and does.

There is another aspect to this name that might be less obvious to some. The word Hadi comes from the root Huda (هدى) in Arabic and has multiple meanings. In addition to guidance, it also means calm and is connected to the word for gift. During my childhood, the more dominant definition due to daily use would have been calm.

I've always found Arabic beautiful and powerful in its storytelling. Within every Arabic word there is a story within its roots, as if saying you can never erase or forget us. The stories that live in words themselves can never be forgotten, even if people speak that language or if the language lives within another language.

There is a calm that comes with true guidance and following The Right Path. When our values align, we are at peace within ourselves and with everything beyond us. Even when making certain decisions that are met with violence and harm, they are still calmer than doing things that move us away from The Right Path.

The Guidance is one of the greatest gifts we can ever receive. It is a gift that can not be quantified. Good advice is to be coveted. The level of guidance we refer to from Allah is beyond anything we can imagine. No level of gratitude is worthy of it, but Allah is also The Most Generous and gives us unrestrictedly.

93 An-Noor: The Light

This name is self-explanatory in many ways.

The word Inara, which comes from the word Noor, is a word that I have used for two large projects post-Oct 7th, 2023. The first was an anthology by queer and trans-Palestinians about a free Falasteen. The second is a queer and trans-Muslim peer support line. The word Inara is the action of lighting. I bring Inara into this space because Allah is The Light, all Light. There is no light anywhere without Allah. Allah is The One Who Lights.

In *Secrets of Divine Love*, A Helwa talks about Heaven and Hell within the context of Light, saying that hell is moving away from The Light — from Allah.

"Heaven and Hell are not only physical manifestations, they are also states of being that reflect what it feels like for the spirit to be close to or

distant from the Divine. In essence, Heaven and Hell are like mirrors that reflect back to us our soul's relationship with God."
— A. Helwa, *Secrets of Divine Love: A Spiritual Journey into the Heart of Islam*

She uses an example of being away from a person we love most dearly — it physically hurts. How painful must it be to be away from The Light?

To me, The Light is liberation. The Light is utopia. The Light is love, compassion, hope – dozens of the other names of The Light. Turning away from liberation, from utopia, from love, from compassion, is moving away from The Light.

The 99 names of Allah map out The Right Path as they tell us who is Allah. The 99 names are not names, they are a roadmap to how we may live wholehearted lives that do not begin or end with our breath in this world. We are so much more than a single lifetime in a single timeline.

3 Ar-Raheem: The Most Compassionate/The All Merciful & 2 Ar-Rahman: The Most Merciful/The Almighty

I had to sit with Al-Rahman and Al-Raheem for a while, allowing them to sit in my body and ask how they differ. The roots for both words are the same: Ra-ha-meem, the same word for uterus in Arabic, رَحِم. I have a lot of thoughts around that last connection, especially because it is often used in sexist ways by cis-men and trans exclusionary ways by cis-women. Every TERFy (Trans Exclusionary Radical Feminist) Muslim organization over uses these two words to solidify that true women have uteruses, and women with uteruses are the only ones who have forgiveness within their hearts.

Al-Raheem is mentioned 114 times, while Al-Rahman is mentioned 57 times.

The name Al-Rahman is also the name of a chapter in the Quran that starts with the following verses:

ٱلرَّحْمَٰنُ ١ عَلَّمَ ٱلْقُرْآنَ ٢ خَلَقَ ٱلْإِنسَٰنَ ٣ عَلَّمَهُ ٱلْبَيَانَ ٤

1) The Most Merciful 2) Taught the quran 3) Created humanity 4) taught them speech

The chapter continues with various incredible things that Al-Rahman has done for us. All of the examples are large scale gifts of creation all around us. Al-Rahman has gifted us everything that we have and will ever know.

Al-Raheem, on the other hand, is used as a reminder that Al-Raheem is The Most Merciful, no matter what actions we take along the way. Al-Raheem is a reminder that our journeys are valid. Al-Raheem is directly in response to the reality that we are meant to make mistakes along the way. We're already perfect when we continue to grow and move towards The Right Path.

Balance is a key part of Islam and any other spiritual pathway. If we stop growing, we stop being human. Without Al-Raheem, we are always set up for failure. Instead, Al-Rahman and Al-Raheem are statements that we are forgiven after messing up as long as we continue on The Right Path. Forgiveness lines our paths guiding us back towards The Right Path even as we stray from it sometimes.

Every human is born with mercy in their heart. Mercy is a part of what makes us human. We make mistakes, we make amends, we forgive and are forgiven. To assume that a uterus is what validates this journey exclusively for some people is to buy into the narratives of systemic oppression around us, which imply that to be human is to not be merciful. Within systems of oppression forgiveness is seen as if it's unnatural. Within systems of oppression, the bar of what it means to be human is so low. Kindness, love, support, mercy are all seen as if we've done something so incredibly beyond our nature. Our nature is mercy, support, love, and kindness. We are the bar that systems of oppression want us to forget has existed for thousands of years.

80 At-Tawab: The Ever Accepting of Repentance

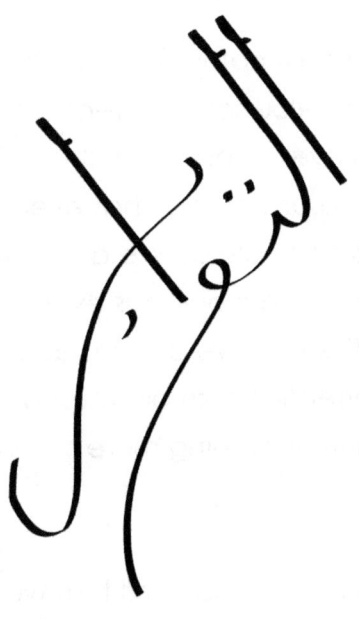

I think it's only hard for humans to accept that we are imperfect — everything else knows that we are. I don't think trees look at us and go, "wow, what a perfect species!" In fact, if anything, every other living being knows how horrid we can be.

The Ever Accepting of Repentance knows that we act with trash behavior, always imperfect, and knows what we're truly capable of. The level of good we are able to do when we are truly on The Right Path is indescribable. We are capable of anything, both the good and the bad.

The philosopher Terance says that nothing human is foreign to any of us. Maya Angelou says in direct response that within her lives every ingredient, the worst and the best.[3] Everything any human has ever done is something we are all capable of. We are capable of the best or worst that anyone has ever done. But we do not get to the best we are capable of without the layers of imperfection that allow us to grow day in and day out. There is nothing more beautiful than growth.

The Ever Accepting of Repentance knows all that we are and can be. Even the Angels questioned our creation, knowing all the evil and harm we can cause. Yet, we were still created. It is not about the harm we cause, or even the worst of evils. It is rather about whether or not we move towards accountability and doing better everyday. This is not to excuse any harm. The opposite is true actually. When we acknowledge that harm is real and accountability is possible, then we have a path to follow: The Right Path.

---

[3] https://www.youtube.com/watch?v=ePodNjrVSsk

79 Al-Barr: The Source of All Goodness and Kindness

This name seems pretty obvious. The Right Path is everything good, but not in the same sense of the "good" we know. What we define as good is complex due to the human experience. Even with an objectively good action, we may inadvertently trigger someone, or, worse: they could be harmed by someone else due to our kindness. For example, interfering in cases of domestic violence could lead to someone being killed immediately after. Even the best of actions could have disastrous consequences.

Allah's kindness is different — it is pure, and whether we know it or not, it is always the absolute best for us. The Source of All Goodness and Kindness cannot be subjective, misinterpreted, or the source of any kind of harm.

The Right Path moves us towards this reality, where our goodness and kindness become more and more accessible, but never fully quite there. No matter how expansive our good is, it'll never be able to encompass everyone's reality — only Al-Barr encompasses everything in existence.

Afterword

Why is it important for Allah to be revealed to us? Allah does not benefit from our recognition. We do not harm Allah through disbelief and violence. Why then is it important for us to know The Divine?

Within each of us lies every ingredient needed for limitless possibilities in how we live our lives. Within each of us exists the ingredients to enact genocide, and within each of us exists the ingredient to inspire joy and love and compassion. We have every possibility built into our DNA — we choose what to do with those possibilities and make them a reality.

There are reminders of The Divine all around us. These reminders extend from reflections in a mirror, the oceans and forests, the depth of valleys, the bitter cold of a desert at night, in every living being, in the stars above us, on the land we're on. The Divine is closer to us than our jugular vein and encompasses everything beyond it.

The Divine teaches us to claim the ingredients that move us towards The Divine, towards the land, and towards one another. The Divine grants us purpose, a direction to move towards when all directions are available to us. The 99 Names of Allah (in all the ways that they have shown up throughout our existence) are a pathway for living our lives. As a species that believes that what is right and wrong is subjective, The Names offer guidance and clarity, recognizing that what moves us towards The Divine is right and what moves us away from The Divine is wrong.

There is a lot that can be said about how The Divine has been weaponized to move us away from The Divine for the short term benefit for a few, but that can only occur when we do not have access to ways of knowledge that affirm our connection with The Divine. There is a reason that at every stage of religious corruption, those in power will punish education, community conversations, questions that ask beyond what they themselves have determined as right or wrong. The Divine asks us, as individuals and communities, to interrogate this compass of morality through these names again and again as we live our lives. The Divine has given us a blueprint and free will to determine how we move through our lives. Free will does not imply being absolved of consequence, for our actions have consequences in this life and in what comes next. The Divine, through these names, made our purpose (steward the land and care for one another) and the paths to achieve this purpose (community care, love, compassion, non-attachment, understanding humanity and divinity (power)) clear. The Divine also made it abundantly clear that we are all connected (every living being, not just humans), and that every step we take on any path impacts everyone and everything.

Our purpose is not an individual one — it can only be completed collectively.

Everything comes from The Divine (Al-Ahad and Al-Samad).

Only Allah creates and is Original (Al-Badi and Al-Musawer).

If Allah wills it it shall be — no one supersedes The Divine (Power)(Al-Qahhar).

Allah has embedded all creation with the essence of The Divine (love, patience, forgiveness, grace, majesty).

Allah has tasked us with roles and responsibilities (stewarding the land and caring for one another)(collectivism)(Al-Jami).

Allah has given us glimpses into things that are beyond us — Only Allah Knows All (non-attachment)(Al-Aleem).

So, where do we go from here? Where do you go from here?

Ideally, now you live. Dreaming and building a better world are not separate things from living. Life is the eating and sleeping and organizing and celebrating and listening and witnessing and giving and taking and gratefulness and love and all the emotions and hoping and connecting and dying. All of life.

The 99 Names of Allah taught me how to live my life, to be collectivist, to be strategic, to envision utopia, to love and be loved, to support and be supported, to move through my emotions, to witness others through their experiences and emotions, and to breathe.

Take a deep breath and live.

Acknowledgments

Immense gratitude to everyone who has inspired my spiritual journey.

A heartfelt thank you to my parents for raising me in a household that prioritized connecting with spirit and allowed me to explore who I am as a spiritual being.

Immense gratitude goes out to the culture workers at the forefront of building a world where fascism is not around the corner.

Special thanks to Noon and Ave for their thoughtful insights and reflections! Immense gratitude to George Ramirez for his artistic direction.

Special thanks to Khaled and Andrea for editing and formatting the book.

Immense gratitude to everyone conducting work that may never be witnessed but is felt every day!

About the Author

Yaffa (they/them) is a stand-up comedian currently withholding their comedy until Falasteen is free. In the meantime, they have vowed to flood the market with books, visual art, and perhaps even plays.

They are an acclaimed disabled, autistic, trans, queer, Muslim, Indigenous Palestinian. Mx. Yaffa is the Executive Director of the Muslim Alliance for Sexual and Gender Diversity (MASGD) and the founder of several non-profits and community projects.

They are multi-generationally displaced and currently searching for the next country to move to. They currently split their time between Jordan and Occupied Lisjan territory, where they are in service to Indigenous communities until they can return home to Falasteen.

About Meraj Publishing

Meraj Publishing is a Trans and Queer Muslim publishing house that centers TQM voices from the global majority, with a focus on Palestinian and Black Authors. Recognizing the vast inequities in the publishing industry, we aim to enable TQM individuals from the global majority to fully own our stories. Meraj prioritizes stories that focus on building utopia, hope, love, spirituality, and belonging. Meraj Publishing is entirely run and operated by the TQM global majority.

www.ingramcontent.com/pod-product-compliance
Lightning Source LLC
Chambersburg PA
CBHW071109160426
43196CB00013B/2518